Career Decision Making

Career Decision Making

Jim Riddell / Melvin Whitehurst

Broadman Press
Nashville, Tennessee

Scripture quotations marked NASB are from the *New American Bible*.
Copyright © The Lockman Foundation, 1960, 1962, 1963, 1971, 1972, 1973,
1975. Used by permission.

Footnotes have not been used in this book. Any book or author quoted
or mentioned in the book is listed in the Bibliography.

Library of Congress Catalog Card Number: 78-059317
Dewey Decimal Classification: 371.4
Subject heading: VOCATIONAL GUIDANCE
Printed in the United States of America

Contents

1
What
Am I Going to Do?

What Am I Going to Do?

If you are a young adult who is thinking about college or your first full-time job, then you are faced with a dilemma. You are asking yourself, "What career should I pursue?" Until now your life has centered around home, school, church, and friends. You have not been particularly concerned with a substantial income or the way you are going to spend your time. Your needs have been taken care of and your time for the most part has been structured around school and family responsibilities. But now you are faced with a tough decision, and you want to be sure you can make the right choice.

There is another complicating factor. If you have a commitment to Christ, you will want to know what career he wants you to pursue. If this is true, your question may be, "What does God want me to do with my life?" You have committed your life to God. If you do what he wants you to do, you will be happy and successful. The problem is knowing God's will for your life. It is not a simple matter. God rarely speaks to us in such a way that we hear him giving verbal instructions. Because of this you may become overwhelmed by confusion and doubt. This book will help you work your way through the confusion and doubt and discover the best career for you to enter.

Making a career choice is not an event that happens in an instant and then the question is settled forever. It is a process. Donald Super, a well-known psychologist, believes that career choice is a lifelong process marked by a continuous series of career decisions which push you through various career stages. Super has found that as you learn about yourself and the various career options open to you, you go through three basic career decision stages: (1) the fantasy stage in which you believe you can do anything, (2) the tentative stage in which you begin to analyze yourself in relation to a career, and (3) the realistic stage in which you finally gain the self-understanding and knowledge of the work world necessary to make a career choice. Thus, you can see as you make choices, you open up certain career alternatives and eliminate others. By doing this you will eventually come to a compromise between what you want in a career and what you can realistically enter. The smaller the compromise between what you want and what you can get, the more effective your career choice. Many experts on career development say that when you have an occupation you want and the compromise is small, you will function more effectively not only in your chosen occupation but also as a person in society.

In making a career choice, then, you are really thinking about a process that contains a long series of decisions, and each decision molds and shapes the direction of your career. It is vitally important to be aware of the kinds of decisions you are making. You simply cannot leave career choice to chance. If you do, you let chance control your destiny. It is better to make a careful examination of your values, abilities, goals, and interpersonal skills in order to relate these things to specific occupations. This book will help you get hold of some of these important career factors and perhaps help you avoid a lifelong series of poor career decisions. *What we are suggesting is hard work.* It requires considerable time and effort. It means that to control your career choice you must make the maximum effort to find out which career will help you fulfill your potential. If you are not ready to make this kind of effort, perhaps you should reassess your Christian commitment. We know that God wants only your best effort.

How Do I Know What God Wants Me to Do?

There are many ideas about responding to God's calling for your life. Most of these ideas are valid but have either been taken to extremes or have been oversimplified. Three basic theories exist that describe how God uses men in his service.

The first theory is that God has created us and given us certain abilities and potential. Beyond this God has no say-so about how we utilize these abilities and potentials. We are free to do as we wish as long as we hold to certain Christian principles. The problem with this point of view is that it says, "God, you do your thing and I'll do mine." There is no relationship with God in addition to no sense of responsibility to God.

The second theory contends that God calls all men to a specific vocation with a special plan for every person's life. All one has to do is plug into this plan and the problems of career choice are solved. Although this plan is acceptable to a certain degree, it has its limits. For one thing it severely hinders the individual's freedom as a person and a Christian. It also makes God's will a big mystery. This theory is attractive because very few decisions are required. All a person has to do is follow the directions, and happiness and success are assured.

The third point of view appears to be somewhat more accurate. In this point of view, God calls all men to be Christians. Furthermore, he gives abilities to many for special Christian work, calling a few to specific religious tasks. This theory expresses the mainstream of thought among the Christian community today and also reflects more accurately the total biblical pattern. Look at the following examples.

Abraham readily comes to mind. Abraham was called into a relationship with God first. The relationship centered around Abraham's obedience to God's commands. We think of Abraham as the father of the Jewish nation. But Abraham's daily work involved being a shepherd. God called Abraham in the midst of his day-to-day world to live and work in a special place and to become the father of a specific nation. Abraham was called to faith first and to a special task second.

On the other hand, there are countless numbers of biblical personalities who played virtually no special role other than to live their lives within the context of their relationship with God. Abraham's son Isaac played no special role other than to be the father of Jacob. Many others in the Bible responded to the message of Christ even though they were not among the twelve apostles.

God calls us all to be committed Christians, living our lives within the realm of his love. He calls some to perform certain tasks. To clarify this concept further, think for a few moments about the kind of relationship which exists between God and committed Christians. There are many symbols given in the Scriptures to describe this relationship. They include Master-servant, Father-child, and Teacher-disciple. Look at the diagram which pictures this partnership.

Focusing on the father-child or master-servant models tends to emphasize a relationship where the person has no ability to make decisions and has no freedom of choice. The father-child relationship, however, expresses the loving relationship between God and ourselves. The master-servant picture expresses a commitment to him, to his message, and to his kingdom.

In the teacher-disciple relationship an emphasis is placed on refining, developing, and putting to work ones abilities. More concisely, the relationship we are proposing is not one like a puppet which has no life other than the puppet's operator. We are suggesting a divine partnership wherein the senior partner establishes a partnership, sets guidelines, and provides challenge for the task by allowing us to put our abilities to work. This is what Paul meant when he said, "We are co-laborers with God," (1 Cor. 3:9, authors' translation). It becomes easy to see Abraham in this light. David is seen as a man after

God's Partnership with You

Creator
Father
Lord
Caller
Enabler

God

To Divine
Partnership

He calls man in to being
He calls man into a relationship
He loves man as a father
He gives man a potential

• • • • • • • •

We respond to his call
We commit ourselves as servant
We love him as a father
We are fulfilled as humans
  by being and doing what God
  has created us to do

creature
child
servant
called
enabled

**Redeemed
Man**

God's heart. Peter, Paul, and all the New Testament figures can be seen this way as well.

You can now see what the statement of God calling all men to Christianity and all Christians to lifelong commitment means. God provides gifts to many for Christian service and calls a few to special tasks. Within the context of our divine partnership with him, we are able to become a part of God's mission in the world.

Another issue worthy of discussion is the difference between work in the secular world and work as opposed to full-time Christian service. If we hold to our third theory, the issue may be answered in terms of our abilities. If God gives an individual certain abilities best utilized within the church, that is where they should be used. This may be as a church vocation or in partial involvement as a committed member of the body of Christ.

Looking at the situation from the other side, if particular abilities are not evident for a specific full-time church-related vocation, a person must not in any way feel like a second-class Christian. There is no separation between those in the ministry and those not in the ministry. God calls persons to specific missions in life: to high moral living, to patience and suffering, and to faithful service. Because individuals have different talents, it is up to each person to combine them in unique ways for the most productive use. God wants each of us to contribute in the best possible way for the advancement of his work.

There are opportunities for Christian service in every occupation. You may become a pastor or become involved in some other religious occupation and contribute to the advancement of God's work. You may contribute just as much in a nonreligious occupation. A postal worker, fire fighter, attorney, plumber—all have opportunities to carry out the mission God lays out for them.

We are all part of God's kingdom. Every person who responds to God's call is a minister. In finding an occupation which will allow us to fulfill our mission as a minister of the Christian faith, we should look at all the possible alternative careers first. It is important to be reasonably certain the occupation you have chosen will provide you with a maximum opportunity for Christian service.

Here is an example of a person who achieved the mission of Christ through a nonreligious occupation. Ralph was a postman. He worked hard to be the best postman possible. He carried letters throughout the neighborhood at a fast business-like pace. Occasionally, he met some of his customers, but he rarely took time to stop and talk. He simply said a friendly hello and moved on quickly. As time passed, people grew to respect his dependable, efficient manner in performing his job. Everyone, sooner or later, learned his name. He developed a sense of respect from those he served. His life was seen as one of happiness and contentment in doing a job well. Because of this respect, some people were even able to stop Ralph long enough to get to know him, at least superficially. Of course, Ralph was not afraid to tell of his Christian convictions.

Responding to God's call in an occupation is very simple. It is a day-to-day dedication to do the best job in whatever occupation you are while all the time remembering the mission God has for you. As long as you are attempting to do your best in an occupation, you will come to learn your strengths and weaknesses, what you can do best, and how to use your life as a Christian minister. Those people who do not follow this philosophy tend to become unhappy in their work, developing various kinds of conflicts on the job, and often become unproductive Christians.

Those who follow God's will by preplanning for an occupation and then performing the occupation to its utmost will be well rewarded. Psychologist Abraham Maslow for years studied the characteristics of people who had extremely good mental health. He found without exception that these persons had a job they felt was important and were totally committed to doing their best. From this we may conclude that one of the major ingredients for happiness and mental well-being is having the best possible job for your talents and performing it with all your energy.

To better understand the importance of finding and performing well in an occupation, you must see the whole picture of what Christ has laid out for you. You should study the Scriptures so you can begin to see how each person's life fits into the total scheme of things. When you understand the significance of each person's contribution, no matter how small or obscure, it is easier for you to begin to make the hard decision of career choice.

Styles of Career Planning

Career choice and career development is becoming increasingly difficult. According to Alvin Toffler in his book, *Future Shock,* the rapid advancements in technology have created a multitide of occupations that were nonexistent a few years ago. For example, the computer programming field did not exist twenty years ago. Transistors and integrated circuits have been developed only in the last fifteen years. Toffler goes on to describe how, through mass communications such as television, we are exposed to many different life-styles and value systems which open up our awareness to many different kinds of career alternatives. If you want to make a good career choice, you must be able to sort through the overchoice of occupations.

To deal with this situation, all people, over a period of time, develop a basic belief on how to go about choosing a career. This belief is perhaps one of the most important considerations in beginning to explore potential careers.

Some people believe that if they wait long enough a career suited to their taste will come along. They are what psychologists call *externals.* They do not want to take the responsibility for choosing. It is easier to always blame circumstances or fate for their failure to come to grips with the difficult choice of an occupation. Externals usually have a history of not developing their potential.

An external belief is expressed often among Christians who passively sit back and wait for God to reveal his will for them. They bide their time, waiting for an open-door or a call to special service. They have faith God will reveal his will to them or will provide the right circumstances to do his will. The problem here is that externals rely too much on emotions and chance. They fail to utilize what God has already given them in terms of abilities and talents. The parable of the talents gives an example. Three men were given talents to use while their master was away. The third man failed because he buried his talent and did not use the talent he had been given.

At the opposite side of this belief are those who believe they can do anything regardless of circumstances. They do not take into account anything but their own personal desires and wishes. It is easier for them to deal only with their feelings than it is to look at reality. Psychologists call these people *internals*. Abilities, goals, values, and personal skills are unimportant to internals. To better describe this belief, consider the young person who wants so much to go into the ministry. He makes a commitment to do so but has a hard time getting along with people or cannot bear to get up in front of a group of people to speak. You see, one must not only come to terms with individual abilities but also to learn to accept limitations.

Those who possess the third basic belief about career choice are the ones who examine both internal and external factors. They are very *realistic*. They have a strong desire to find out what career is best for them. They possess a high degree of motivation that will enable them to see the whole process through. In short, these people have commitment as well as a realistic sense of the complexity and difficulty of choosing a career. We hope you are among this group because if you are not you may have difficulty motivating yourself to complete this book.

To help assess your readiness to explore career alternatives, complete the following questionnaire. Circle yes for all the statements with which you agree. Circle no for all the statements with which you disagree. Remember many of the statements are true, but please express what best fits your understanding of the statement.

CAREER STYLE SURVEY

Yes No   1. Career choice is mostly dependent on being in the right place at the right time.

Yes No   2. There is only one career that is right for each person.

Yes No   3. If you wait long enough. the right career will come along.

Yes No   4. Most career planning is useless because most people will wind up taking whatever job is available at the time they are looking for a job.

Yes No   5. If I wait long enough, God will show me what his will is for my life.

Yes No   6. God has a special task for each person.

Yes No   7. A person can do any job if they only try hard enough.

Yes No   8. A person who is motivated to succeed will always succeed.

Yes No   9. One should be careful about talking to other people about careers because they will probably unintentionally try to influence you to go into the same career they are in.

Yes No 10. A person should decide on the ideal job first and not worry about values, abilities, or goals.

Yes No 11. Once God has called you to a career you must pursue it regardless of the obstacles.

Yes No 12. Only God will help you to overcome personal deficiencies.

Yes No 13. A person should strongly consider values, goals, and abilities when choosing a career.

Yes No 14. Most people would have more control over

their career if they were willing to invest considerable time in career exploration.

Yes No 15. People should plan for a career well in advance.

Yes No 16. People should consider more than one alternative when they are making career choices.

Yes No 17. God has already shown me part of his will by giving me certain talents.

Yes No 18. God has several opportunities for me to serve and gives me a choice of how I want to serve.

Summary of Interpretation

A. Number of yeses on questions 1-6   _____
   Number of nos on questions 1-6   _____
B. Number of yeses on questions 7-12   _____
   Number of nos on questions 7-12   _____
C. Number of yeses on questions 13-18   _____
   Number of nos on questions 13-18   _____

In which category did you have the largest number of yeses? If it is category A, then your basic career belief system is external. If it is category B, it is internal. If it is category C, your belief system is realistic.

If your orientation is realistic, we feel you are right on target. If not, you should stop and decide if you are really ready to pursue a program of career exploration.

Can I Really Choose the Right Occupation?

One of the major problems young adults have in making career decisions is being sure of making the right decision. Can you make the right choice? Our answer to that question is a strong yes. But we feel there are certain things you must resolve. God gives you the basic abilities and talents to achieve in many different kinds of occupations. He has confidence in you and your ability to perform well. What he wants you to do is act on what he has given you.

You must understand that you will rarely have a clear revelation of God's will for your life. There will inevitably be some questions of lingering doubt about what is the right course of action. If you allow these doubts to hold you up, you will be afraid to take action. Acting on the basis of leadership that comes from prayer, Bible study, and assessment of your personal talents is an act of faith. Demanding some kind of sign or a clear indication of God's will can cause you never to fulfill your career potential.

People often choose not to decide about a career. They become confused by the fear of having to make a decision. It is easier to put off a decision than to run the risk of failing. They say, "Why choose and face failure when you can put off the inevitable." Perhaps through some combination of circumstances something will occur to make the decision for this nondecider. This rarely if ever happens, however.

In summary, it is essential that a career decision maker understand the following concept:

God Has a Plan

The Plan Is to Christianize the World

Your Role Is to Use Your Unique Talents to Contribute to God's Plan

Look at the following three boxes. Each box has an age range. List as many things as you can remember that you did during these age ranges to contribute to God's plan. Keep in mind that you did not have to be doing direct church-related activities.

Age-Span Chart

Age 10-15	Age 16-20	Age 21+

By looking over your activities during these age spans, you should begin to get some ideas as to the kinds of things you do best in helping carry out God's plan. Do these activities involve working with others? Are they activities which can be developed into a full-time career? Ponder these questions for a few moments. To help you better understand this, we want you to write a paragraph describing the story of your life. Be certain to include how you believe you have contributed to God's plan.

Summary of Life

Look back over the age-span chart and paragraph. List ten things you would like to contribute to God's plan in your lifetime. Think about ideal contributions. That is, if you could contribute anything to God's plan, what ten things would you do? This may not be easy for you to do. You may have to spend considerable time thinking about it or talking with someone about it. Work hard to list all ten things before you continue.

Things I Want to Contribute to God's Plan	Rank
1.	
2.	
3.	
4.	
5.	
6.	
7.	
8.	
9.	
10.	

Now go back and rank each contribution in order of importance. Pick the four contributions you are most committed
to achieving and list them below in the commitment box.

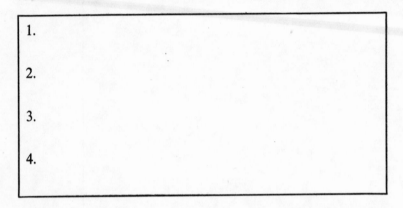

1.

2.

3.

4.

Of course these four commitments are important to you.
They are the things which you can personally contribute. Actually putting these commitments into practice is another story
though. No matter how hard you try to do these things, there
will always be barriers to hold you back. The point is you
will have to work hard to carry out these commitments, and
a career which fully uses your potentials will greatly increase
your chances of fulfilling these commitments.

2
Who Am I?

Discerning God's will for your life as it relates to your career decisions involves knowing yourself,—coming to terms with your abilities, strengths, and limitations. It also involves knowing something about your spiritual pilgrimage and your sense of religious mission.

Matthew 25 gives the parable of the man who left on a long journey. Before leaving he called three of his servants to him and left them responsible for some talents. The servants were to use these talents in order to gain a profit for the owner. Two men doubled what was given to them. The third, however, merely buried what was given to him. Several facts can be surmised from this parable. Every person has certain abilities; each person is responsible for using these abilities in such a manner that will bring a profit to the master; and the abilities given vary in amount and kind. Reward is given on the basis of how well you utilize what has been given to you. If your common goal is to do the work of God in the world, telling his message in word and deed, then you must filter out the traits that you have which make you unique.

Barnabas and Paul are examples of different gifts being put to work. Barnabas was not known as a great preacher. He was known as a comforter, an advocate for the underdog, and one who was dependable and not apt to have his mind changed easily. He got along well with people. When a radical young Pharisee was converted to Christianity, none of the Christians would have anything to do with him because they were afraid of him. But Barnabas took him to one side, listened to his story, and then presented him to the church. Later

Barnabas took Saul to help him teach the new Christians in Antioch. Eventually these two launched out on a missionary trip that saw Paul come into his own as a missionary, preacher, and teacher.

Paul, on the other hand, was a highly trained theologian, a strong and extremely able preacher, a relentless and tireless worker who never fell back even when facing opposition and antagonism. Not only that, he was born away from Palestine, was born a Roman citizen, and grew up in a cosmopolitan environment. All of which uniquely suited him to the role of missionary in a Roman world.

Paul and Barnabas were radically different in their style, approach, and attitude, yet each had a significant role to play in the course of biblical history. It took a man like Paul to launch the missionary movement of the early church, but it took a man like Barnabas to bring him into the church and to help him develop his gifts to be used in order for him to begin his missionary career.

One other person who bears mentioning is Mark, the writer of the Gospel of Mark. Mark was the nephew of Barnabas. He was a younger man who had known some of the twelve apostles and had most likely seen or known Jesus during his earthly ministry. Mark was invited to join Barnabas and Paul on their missionary journey. He went along as an assistant and was probably used to tell the new Christians about the life and ministry of Jesus. However, about halfway through the journey, Mark for no apparent reason, went home to Jerusalem. Paul saw this as a failure on the part of Mark. Mark could not stay with the work. He was not reliable, and he was not committed. Later when Paul and Barnabas were planning a second trip, they had a sharp argument over whether or not to take Mark along. The result was that Barnabas and Mark went one direction while Paul took Silas and went another direction. Mark later is the one who writes what is acknowledged by many as the first written account of Christ's ministry.

Romans 12:4-8; 1 Corinthians 12:28-29; and Ephesians 4:11 give some lists of varying gifts. These all relate to the areas of responsibility within the church. In each instance the emphasis is upon the need for each individual to exercise his gift in such a fashion as to aid and assist in the furtherance of God's work through the church. These lists of abilities can in no way be considered all the gifts of God.

Do you have an unusual ability to listen to people? Do you naturally enjoy meeting people? Do you have that special ability to lead others? In essence—do you know yourself? You must know yourself if you are to make appropriate career decisions. You must know what you like and dislike, what you feel in various life situations, how your relationships with others affect your life, and your basic abilities. This may sound like an easy task. However, humans are interesting and complex creatures, and all of these self-knowledge factors constantly change with time and circumstances. It is important to see yourself as a changing, emerging individual that never stays exactly the same for long. As a result, you must be continuously looking at your changing self so you will not get lost in the past or blinded by the future.

It is difficult to see yourself as you really are. Many people get caught up in being something they either want to be or something created by mass media. They try to live by an idealistic standard created by society. Don E. Hamcheck describes this dilemma in his book *Encounters with the Self:* "We look in the mirror hoping for an image of what we want to be only to be disappointed when it simply reflects what we are." If you fail to look at yourself realistically, all your career decisions will be based on inaccurate assumptions. These assumptions will tend to add up over a long period of time which will most likely cause you to feel miserable and regretful of the way you spent your life. Those who do this will pay the unfortunate price of a lifetime of unhappiness and loneliness that comes from failing to fully realize their potential.

Some people shy away from any kind of self-exploration

for fear of finding out something bad about themselves. They develop all kinds of rationalizations on why they should not make a concerted attempt to look at themselves objectively. Sometimes they say they simply don't have the time. At other times, they downplay or ridicule self-exploration as useless. Any way you look at it, those people who have a basic understanding of who they are almost always make better career decisions.

To ultimately find the career which helps you fulfill your potential, you must answer these three very important questions:

Who am I?
Where am I going?
How do I get there?

In this chapter we are going to help you examine the first question, Who am I? If you know yourself, you are almost assured of finding the answers to the questions: Where am I going? How do I get there?

We are now going to help you examine four important areas of self-understanding. We believe that you should clearly understand these areas before you proceed to other areas of career decision making. We will ask you to make an intense investigation of these four areas. The four areas of self-exploration that we are going to explore are:

- How do you see yourself in the present?
- What kinds of interpersonal relationships do you have?
- How well do you communicate?
- How well do you understand your basic abilities?

How Do You See Yourself in the Present?

Some people live predominantly in the past. Still others live predominantly for the future. In both cases these individuals are avoiding a very important part of their life—the present. Living predominantly for either the past or future tends to retard your ability to make career decisions. When you are able to live fully in the present, you have a better chance to utilize the past and future in planning your career. In this part we will focus on the "here and now" in an effort to help you see yourself in the present.

We want you to write a brief description of the following topics. Write the description as it relates to you at the present time. Focus on being as objective as possible. That is, try to look at your situation as it really is rather than how you want it to be. Describe carefully how you actually see yourself in these areas.

Relationships with friends

Relationships with family members

How others view you

Understanding of your personal meaning in life

The type of Christian example you provide to others

Now we are going to ask you to explore several critical issues in your life. Provide only brief answers. Try to be direct and to the point.

What are your three greatest fears at the present time?

1.

2.

3.

What is the biggest single struggle that you have in your life at the present?

If you could acquire five things that would bring you happiness, what would they be?

1.

2.

3.

4.

5.

Name one thing you would have to do to obtain each of these five things.

1.

2.

3.

4.

5.

What are three things you would like to learn about yourself?

1.

2.

3.

What Kinds of Interpersonal Relationships Do You Have?

Your relationships with others have an important effect on the kind of person you ultimately become and on the kind of career you eventually choose. Robert Weiss and his associates at Harvard Medical School studied the lives of people uprooted by broken marriages, retirement, and moving substantial distances from their home. From these studies they concluded that people need human relationships to increase their sense of well-being. Thus, human relationships serve a very important function in career decision making.

Weiss and his associates identified several categories of relationships which seem to be necessary. We will ask you to explore four of these kinds of human relationships.

1. *Knowing people who share our concerns.* As we live, we develop common concerns with our acquaintances. These shared concerns are important in preventing us from developing a feeling of social isolation and the accompanying feelings of boredom and meaninglessness.

2. *Knowing people we can depend on in a pinch.* In the past we have been able to depend on relatives for this kind of relationship, but with increased mobility in our society and the increased dispersion of families across the United States we are forced to find others to assist us in a time of need. If we do not have these kinds of relationships, we may develop a sense of anxiety and vulnerability.

3. *Having one or more really close friends.* We must have one or more close friends with whom we can share our innermost feelings. They must be people to whom we have ready

access. According to Weiss, such relationships serve the vital function of providing us with our need for intimacy. Without intimate relationships we may experience a deep sense of loneliness.

4. *Knowing people who respect our competence.* We need these kinds of relationships to reassure us about our self-worth. We may gradually win the respect of fellow workers or respect from achieving a successful family life, and so on. Thus, the absence of this kind of relationship greatly decreases our self-esteem.

Now let's explore these four kinds of relationships with respect to your own life.

Knowing People Who Share Our Concerns

List below any organization in which you are currently a member. Beside each organization name the primary concern you are expressing by being a member of this organization.

Organization	*Concern*
1.	
2.	
3.	
4.	
5.	
6.	
7.	

In the past two years you have probably attended some meetings concerning local or national issues or issues you felt were important. List any of the meetings below and state your primary concern being expressed.

Meeting	*Concern*
1.	
2.	
3.	

4.
5.

If you did not attend any meetings, list some of the meetings held in the last two years which express your personal concerns.

Meeting	*Concern*
1.	
2.	
3.	
4.	
5.	

What are your major concerns in life at the moment?
1.

2.

3.

4.

5.

List five people you know who share your major concerns.
1.
2.
3.
4.
5.

Knowing People We Can Depend on in a Pinch

If you were to become ill, who do you think would be personally concerned? List several people and reason they would be concerned.

Concerned Person	*Reason They Are Concerned*
1.	
2.	
3.	
4.	
5.	

If you needed someone to check your house daily for a week while you were on vacation with your family, who could you depend on?

1.
2.
3.
4.
5.

If you had an emergency need of $200 until payday next week, who are some people you would ask for a loan?

1.
2.
3.
4.
5.

Having One or More Really Close Friends

Name five people you regard as close friends.

1.
2.
3.
4.
5.

Do you sometimes wish you had more personal friends? Explain your answer below.

When (or if) you have a problem in the following areas, with which friends would you probably talk? Name one person beside each area.

Career Decision _____

Religion _____

Feeling Lonely _____

Feeling Depressed _____

State your definition of a friend below.

Knowing People Who Respect Our Competence

Name three people who respect your competence in each of the following areas.

As a student
1.
2.
3.

As a Christian
1.
2.
3.

As a friend
1.
2.
3.

As a decision maker
1.
2.
3.

How competent do you feel as a person? Answer this below.

What has happened that makes you feel competent or incompetent? Analyze this carefully below.

You have now completed an analysis of the kinds of interpersonal relationships you have. We have asked you to think through some of the more important kinds of relationships. At this point, you may want to talk with some of your friends or relatives about them. There may be some relationships that you want to improve. In any event, your choice of career and success in that career is largely dependent on the kinds of interpersonal relationships you develop with others.

How Well Do You Communicate?

Communication is an unavoidable aspect of human existence. Whether you want to or not, you are always communicating something to others verbally or nonverbally. Communication is often complex and multifaceted. Miscommunication—one's inability to communicate what they want to communicate—often delays or in some cases destroys personal growth. If you want to enter into and progress in a career, your ability to communicate clearly and concisely will be an absolutely essential skill.

The kind of career you choose will have a close relationship with the way you characteristically communicate with others. For example, if you are an outgoing person who likes to talk with almost anyone you see, the type of career you choose will be greatly enhanced if you are able to utilize this interest in communication. On the other hand, you may be the type who likes to communicate with only a few close associates. A career that thrusts you into a situation where you have to communicate often with new people may cause you great unhappiness and would perhaps even interfere with your career development.

The following thirty statements will help you identify the communication style which is most characteristic of you. After you complete assessing your communication style, we will help you see how this directly affects your career choice. Read each statement carefully and place a check by each statement with which you agree. After doing this, pick the communication style which is most characteristic of you. You may or may not agree with every statement contained in the style you choose. Simply choose the set of statements which seems to fit you best. Keep in mind that each of these three styles of communication is employed successfully by individuals and there is no one best communication style.

Communication Style 1

_____ 1. When talking with a person, I like to deal predominantly with the facts instead of with that person's feelings.

_____ 2. I think it is important to be as logical and realistic as possible when talking with a person about an important matter.

_____ 3. I think that when communicating with a person it is not always necessary for that person to like me. In fact, it is not necessary that anyone like me in order for me to communicate effectively with that person.

_____ 4. Most people's problems are their own making.

_____ 5. When I have a problem with another person, I try to develop a clear solution to the problem.

_____ 6. When I am having a problem with another person, I think it is important to deal with the other person in a direct and forthright manner.

_____ 7. In most cases I do not get upset when another person does not like me.

_____ 8. When I am having an argument with another person, after a while I usually stop and try to analyze the problem.

_____ 9. Overemotional people often use their emotions to try to manipulate others and make others feel uncomfortable enough to give them their way.

_____ 10. To communicate effectively with others a person must take responsibility for the things he or she communicates and avoid blaming others.

Communication Style 2

_____ 1. When someone does something I like, I try to let that person know about it almost immediately.

_____ 2. When people get annoyed at me for no apparent reason, it is probably due to their past negative experiences with someone like me.

_____ 3. Sometimes it is just best to ignore some problems.

_____ 4. It is very important for me to give my friends some sort of gift on very special occasions.

_____ 5. When I have completed a project or activity in which I think I have achieved something, I like to celebrate.

_____ 6. Sometimes I get angry at another person so he will realize that I mean business.

_____ 7. I am very careful to distinguish between words and actions. Actions speak louder than words. What a person does is more important to me than what he says.

_____ 8. When people achieve something, they usually feel better about themselves. People must achieve something significant in their lives in order to have an adequate view of themselves.

_____ 9. When I want another person to do something, the best way is to set up the conditions in which, if they perform as I wish, they will get some sort of reward.

_____ 10. People should look around at all the opportunities which may bring them happiness and then seek to find constructive ways to take advantage of these opportunities.

Communication Style 3

_____ 1. It is extremely important to try to understand others no matter how abnormal their behavior seems to be.

_____ 2. My feelings are more important than anyone else's.

_____ 3. It is not important to try to change yourself or others. It is more important to accept yourself and others.

_____ 4. When talking with another person, I am usually successful in not judging the other person.

_____ 5. When talking with another person, I deal predominantly with that person's feelings instead of the facts.

_____ 6. I find it very rewarding to accept another person with no strings attached, and I try to do this with the people I encounter.

_____ 7. About 99.9 percent of the people will not try to take advantage of you even if given a chance.

_____ 8. Most people try to do what is right even though it may hurt them.

_____ 9. Being oneself is more important than considering your friends' feelings.

_____ 10. I can communicate with others more effectively if I concentrate on understanding myself first instead of understanding the other person.

Add up the number of checks in each communication style. Rank the communication styles.

Rank

Communication Style 1 _____
Communication Style 2 _____
Communication Style 3 _____

Read the following descriptions of each communication style. When you finish, list five possible jobs that would use your top communication style.

Communication Style 1

Those who identified closely with communication style 1 are likely to communicate predominantly with others on the basis of facts and issues. You tend to be very practical and will probably be bugged by those who make illogical decisions. You will often appeal to your friends by reasoning with them. Also you will probably be very careful not to allow emotions to interfere with good communications. You will in most instances be very forthright, assertive, and even aggressive at times when communicating directly with others. You try especially hard to make sense out of what is going on. Many times you may give the appearance of being confident and self-assured. You think sympathy and the "bleeding heart" approach to others is a waste of time. What people really need to do is to stand up for what they believe. People who do not do this will not be your friend for long.

Communication Style 2

In communication style 2 the use of rewards is extremely important. When another person does something to please you, you are quick to compliment him or her. Dates and events are very special, so you usually keep account of the important ones. You have the most fun in celebrating some successful achievement with another. Figuring out ways to advance on the job is usually important to you. You are very good at noticing other peoples' behavior and have a strong belief that friends must help each other or not remain friends. If a person does something you do not like, you usually figure out a way to see that the person is in some way punished. In this style you are always conscious of the rewards in a situation. You may tend to set up situations in which friends can compliment you.

Communication Style 3

Communication style 3 shows a less aggressive and more quiet approach to people. You like to listen first before plunging into a relationship. Other people's feelings are paramount to you. You usually attempt to understand how another person is seeing the situation to the extent that you do not get a chance to put in your point of view. Sometimes you wish you were a little more outgoing. You will probably show anger only on rare occasions. When talking with another person, you will often be thinking about how you feel in relation to the situation. You may be quick to tell others how you feel, but not in an aggressive sense. Aggressive people may often take you to be a passive person. However, you prefer to deal with people in a low-key manner.

After reading the descriptions of the three communication styles, we want you to take your top communication style and list five potential jobs that would allow your style to function.

1.
2.
3.
4.
5.

Although you may have a distinct communication style, the amount and quality of communications may be determined by the way you initiate communications with others. The following is a list of ways one may initiate communication. Check the ones characteristic of you.

Initiating Communication

_____ 1. When I don't understand a statement, I immediately ask for clarification.

_____ 2. I usually speak first when I meet someone.

_____ 3. I usually tell the person how I feel about the situation without being asked.

_____ 4. I am usually firm in stating my position first.

_____ 5. I can communicate better after I have stated my position.

_____ 6. When I don't understand a statement, I usually wait to see if subsequent communications will clear it up.

_____ 7. I usually wait to be asked before I tell someone how I feel.

_____ 8. I usually don't speak first when I meet another person.

_____ 9. It is best to let others state their position before I state my own.

_____10. By hearing another's position first, I can communicate better.

The above statements show whether you are aggressive or casual in initiating communications with another person. The first five statements are considered more aggressive ways of initiating communication, while the last five represent a more casual approach to communication. Determine whether your style is more aggressive or casual.

What kinds of careers do you think require aggressive communicators? List at least three below.

1.

2.

3.

What kinds of careers do you think require casual communicators? List three below.

1.

2.

3.

How Well Do You Understand Your Abilities?

We all have abilities in differing amounts. No person is exactly like another in his abilities. Thus, it is often difficult to understand the unique patterns of these abilities. Usually no one ability is involved in any specific job. Some jobs require a high ability in perhaps one area but in most jobs a person must make use of many different abilities. We are going to define in a limited way some of these specific abilities below so that you can begin to assess your abilities. Read over these abilities carefully. There are ten abilities defined. After you have read them, go back and rank them from 1 to 10 according to what you believe to be your top abilities. Your top ability should be ranked number 1, second to top ability number 2, and so forth.

Abilities

Rank   *Ability*

_____ Verbal Ability: This is the ability to understand and use words. Reading, spelling, grammar, reading comprehension, and writing are involved in verbal abilities.

_____ Numerical Ability: This is the understanding and utilization of math skills or numbers.

_____ Abstract Ability: This is the ability to solve problems or understand ideas where there are no verbal or numerical abilities involved.

_____ Space Relations: This is the ability to see objects in three dimension while looking at them on a flat surface.

_____ Mechanical Ability: This is the ability to work with machines or tools that require maintenance or fixing.

_____ Social Ability: This is the ability to understand and deal with people.

_____ Selling Ability: As the word says, this is the ability to sell or promote ideas or products to other people.

_____ Clerical Ability: This is the ability to efficiently and effectively perform routine clerical and typing activities.

_____ Artistic Ability: The ability to draw or paint pictures.
_____ Musical Ability: The ability to play musical instruments or to perform musical tasks.

Remember, you should have ranked all ten of these abilities according to the abilities you perceived that you possess. Pick your top three abilities and write them in the abilities box.

Abilities Box

```
┌─────────────────────────────────────────────────┐
│                                                 │
│                                                 │
│                                                 │
│                                                 │
│                                                 │
└─────────────────────────────────────────────────┘
```

On the following pages we have listed these ten abilities with several occupations under each. These particular occupations, while requiring several different abilities, will use this ability to a large extent. Look at your top three abilities and the occupations under each one of these abilities. Select one occupation that seems to be the most interesting to you and list them below.

Ability	*Occupation*
1.	
2.	
3.	

VERBAL ABILITY	*SPACE RELATIONS*
Public Relations Worker	Artist
Personnel and Labor	Engineer
Relations Worker	Auto Mechanic
Advertising Worker	Plumber
Writer	Machinist
Teacher	Photographer

VERBAL ABILITY

Real Estate Salesperson
Counselor
Psychologist
Interpreter
Newspaper Reporter
Radio Announcer

SPACE RELATIONS

Diesel Mechanic
Designer
Dentist
Dental Assistant
Dental Hygienist
Architect

NUMERICAL ABILITY

Engineer
Actuary
Machinist
Astronomer
Physicist
Electronics
Computer Programmer
Architect
Radio and TV Repairperson
Accountant

MECHANICAL ABILITY

Aircraft Mechanic
Automotive Mechanic
Carpenter
Truck Driver
Outboard Motor Mechanic
Computer Technician
Machinist
Welder
Bookbinder
Electroplater

ABSTRACT ABILITY

Draftsperson
Writer
Public Relations Worker
Advertiser
Research Scientist
Engineer
Economist
Sociologist
Political Scientist
Newspaper Reporter

SOCIAL ABILITY

City Manager
Bank Teller
Hotel Manager
Credit Manager
Personnel Manager
Teacher
Salesperson
Minister
Social Worker
Psychologist
Public Relations

SELLING ABILITY

Manager
Salesperson
Banker
Advertiser
Interior Designer
Real Estate Worker

MUSICAL ABILITY

Singer
Music Director
Choir Director
Musician

CLERICAL ABILITY

Secretary
Office Manager
Accountant
Bank Clerk
File Clerk
Statistician
Surveyor

ARTISTIC ABILITY

Artist
Engineer
Advertiser
Designer
Architect
Sign Painter
Draftsperson

Although you have briefly assessed some of your basic abilities, you may still have other strengths. Below list your five most important strengths.

1.

2.

3.

4.

5.

Now list your five greatest weaknesses.

1.

2.

3.

4.

5.

We want you to rewrite your weaknesses from a positive point of view. Take the position that each weakness listed above is actually a strength. Rewrite each weakness in a way that makes it a strength.

1.

2.

3.

4.

5.

Summary

In this chapter you have explored some of the important things about yourself that you need to know before looking at other aspects of career development. You have looked at how you see yourself at the present time, explored your interpersonal relationships, looked at your major way of dealing with people through your communication style, and explored your basic abilities and strengths. All of these things will play an important role in your career choice and in your career development.

We are going to ask you to summarize this chapter in capsule form so that you may better understand how these things fit into your career plans.

**Most Important Thing
That Would Bring Me
Happiness**

**What I Can
Do Now To
Bring This to Me**

My Major Concern

**Person Who
Most Shares
This Concern**

**My Major
Communication Style**

**My Major Way
of Initiating
Communication**

My Top Two Abilities

**List Two
Occupations of Interest
From Each Ability**

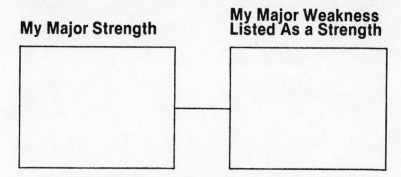

My Major Strength

My Major Weakness Listed As a Strength

To conclude this chapter we want you to write a paragraph using the information in this summary to describe to someone who does not know the kind of person that you see yourself to be. Use all of the information in this summary.

The Way I See Myself

3
What Is Important to Me?

One important step in making a career decision is deciding what is really important to you. Do you want work that is primarily in an office or outdoors? Do you want to work with your hands in a skilled job or would you prefer to work in a managerial position? Do you like working alone or do you want to work around people? The process of deciding what is important to you is called *values clarification*. This process helps you decide what you value in life and what aspects of a potential career you value the most.

Deciding what you value the most can later result in your choosing a career that you will enjoy and will be extemely rewarding and fulfilling for you. This process can also help you eliminate many areas that would not be satisfying to you. Note the following example:

Margie has just graduated from college with a degree in marketing. A company in her hometown offered her an excellent position in sales shortly after she graduated. Margie turned the job down because she was not interested in sales. After four years in college her degree in marketing was not what she wanted.

The reason Margie is in that kind of situation is because she had not clarified what was deeply important to her.

At this point you are probably wondering just exactly what we mean by values. Carl Elder describes a value as something that is desirable or has worth. To value is to rate something highly. You may value freedom, religious beliefs, recognition, wealth, or something else in different degrees than other people. Most people have different values. From the previous chapter we can surmise that Paul felt being an active missionary was most important, while Barnabus felt that caring for people was more important. Although both of these men valued the same thing, they did so in different amounts. So, in understanding your values you must know not only how much you value something, but in what order. Values clarification often becomes a matter of priorities. Look at the following descriptions of two men who had difficulty in deciding on a priority for their values.

Last Sunday during Sunday School class, Joe talked about how important he thought the Christian way of life was for him and anyone willing to follow the teachings of Christ. On Monday Joe was arrested for being drunk and disorderly at a local bar.

John is one of the leaders in the church. His many contributions have helped the church grow and progress. John is also a successful businessman. Last year he was indicted for income tax evasion.

Joe and John definitely had some values conflict. Perhaps their stated values and the values they practiced were not in order. Of course if you examine these two men's lives more closely you would probably find both a lack of understanding of their priorities and a general lack of awareness of their personal values.

From these statements, we can conclude that at the core of our personality is a set of values. These values are our guides to living. Over a period of time we often superimpose other beliefs which serve to cover up or at least mask our true values. Thus, we often act on a mixture of our true values and other values learned from past experiences. When one is able to sift away all the covering and get down to their true values, he will find them to be truly important values that Christ wanted each person to have.

It is not easy to understand your values. You live in a world where the mass media has exposed you to a multitude of lifestyles and value systems. You can easily see people who seem to be living a fabulously glamorous life and people who have reached the very bottom of despair. The confusing thing in all of this is that people now seem to have an overchoice of value systems from which to pick. Sorting through all of these choices, especially with all the rapid changes in our world, can lead to a bewildering outlook on life with inconsistent attitudes and behaviors springing forth within you. If you hedge on understanding your values, the pressures from our fast-paced world and the bombardment of information from the mass media will only serve to compound your doubts about career choice and career development.

Values are your primary motivators. They give you energy for action. You will tend to follow your values or what you believe to be your true values at all costs. Of course, a distorted view of your true values can lead you to many dead-end streets in searching for the right career. If you can match your set of values to a career, your motivation to achieve in that career will be greatly increased. If you do not, you will be filled with self-doubt all along the way. You may wind up like Margie, totally rejecting her four years of education. If you understand your values, many other things fall into place in your career development. Once you have a clear understanding of your values, your choice of career will be greatly simplified. In addition, your behavior will take on a more consistent look. You will be acting and saying the same things. You will not be one person at church and another on the job or at school. You will not have the anxiety of what is right or wrong for you in your career choice.

It is also important to realize that your values will change as you grow and mature and as your life situation changes. As a teenager, independence and self-identity are very prominent; as a young adult, personality creativity ranks very high. Yet as a married person, family life takes on a major priority.

Christianity and Values

One other question you may ask is, "Does my Christianity have any impact on my values?" The answer is yes, especially in the area of your career decisions. The Bible reflects man's efforts to clarify his values in the light of his relationship to his Creator. In the Garden of Eden, man is seen as created in the image of God—innocent, without sin. Yet he is immediately confronted with the need to make a value judgment. He is faced with a decision. Will he value more the command of God and not eat the forbidden fruit, or will he value more the independence of eating the fruit? Later God established his relationship with the nation of Israel based on the law summarized in the Ten Commandments. The Israelites were faced with a value judgment. Do they value their relationship to God and the benefits of that relationship, or do they value more the worship of Baal? Amos the prophet cries out for mercy and justice. In the Sermon on the Mount Jesus says: "Do not be anxious then saying, 'What shall we eat?' or 'With what shall we clothe ourselves?' For all those things do the Gentiles eagerly seek; for your heavenly Father knows that you need all these things. But seek first his kingdom and his righteousness, and all these things shall be added unto you" (Matt. 6:31-33, author's translation).

Later in the first chapter of Romans, Paul first places the greatest value on the gospel of Jesus Christ and then discusses how man, in general, has chosen human wisdom and lust. In Galatians 5, Paul discusses the works of the flesh as well as the fruits of the Spirit. Here he contrasts immorality, impurity, and sensuality with love, joy, peace, patience, and goodness.

A Christian's value system will be the result of his relationship to God. In fact the challenge of the gospel is, Will you value Jesus Christ above all others? Paul often spoke of the contrast between the individual before his conversion and after. As a result of his relationship to God, he had a whole new set of priorities. The primary concern for the Christian is no longer success, pleasure, or power, but love, service, and commitment to the cause of Christ.

It is this kind of new value system that will cause a man like Albert Schweitzer, an accomplished musician with the assurance of a great career, to go back to school at thirty, gain a degree in medicine, and become a medical missionary in order to meet the health needs of the African people. The Christian young person no longer asks, "What am I going to do with the rest of my life?" Rather he asks, "What would God have me do with my life?"

One important task for the Christian is to integrate his value system in such a way that it encompasses his whole life. There cannot be two separate value systems that effect the entirety of his life.

In this chapter we are going to help you clarify your values. We do not want you to change them but simply to have a clear understanding of what is important to you. We are now ready to help you look at your values. We are going to ask you to make an assessment of your values and then make an analysis of your top values.

Values Clarification

List five things about an occupation that are important to you. In other words, if you had the *ideal* occupation, what things would that occupation provide for you? List them below. Think about this carefully before you make this list.

1.

2.

3.

4.

5.

From the following list, pick the three values most important to you in an occupation.

Independence	Creativity
Social service	Achievement
Money	Variety
Challenge	Travel

1.
2.
3.

From the following list of values, pick the three values most important to you.

Service to the church	Prayer
Service to God	Worship
Service to others	Setting a Christian
Day-to-day Christian living	example
Teaching others about Christianity	Bible knowledge

1.
2.
3.

From the following list of values, pick the three values that are most important to you.

To feel important
To live near home
To have high status
To work in a small company
To have a high salary
To be a leader
To work outdoors
To have good working hours

1.
2.
3.

Look at this list of values and pick the three most important values to you.

Work that involves excitement
Work that involves daily changing situations
Working with others
Working with ideas
Working on solving problems
Work where you can set your own pace
Work where you can advance
Work where you are a team member
Work where you help others
Work where you are your own boss
Work where you manage other people
Work where you make something
Work where you design something
Work which requires a high degree of skill with your hands

1.

2.

3.

If only ten inhabitants of the earth were to remain and all others had to leave, list five reasons why you should stay. Don't be modest. Don't be afraid to analyze closely the value of yourself as a person.

1.

2.

3.

4.

5.

From these five reasons, list five values you are expressing.

1.

2.

3.

4.

5.

You now have a list of twenty-two values. Go back and look over all of these values closely. Pick the five values that you believe to be most important to you. List them below *in order of importance.*

1.

2.

3.

4.

5.

On this page write a brief paragraph describing the kind of occupation or work that would help you utilize these values. You do not have to know the exact job, but you are to describe an imaginary kind of occupation.

We are now going to help you analyze your most important values. You are to take each of your top five values and complete a values analysis. This analysis will help you look at how each of these five values has served you and whether the value will continue to influence your career choice in the future. Look at the following chart. On the left-hand side are the numbers from 1 to 10. Estimate the importance of your value during each age span of your life with 10 being the highest and 1 the lowest value. Complete the chart and questions after the chart. There will be five sets so you can complete the in-depth analysis of each value.

Value _____

	0 to 10 yrs.	10 to 15 yrs.	15 to 20 yrs.	20 to 30 yrs.	10 yrs +
10	·	·	·	·	·
9	·	·	·	·	·
8	·	·	·	·	·
7	·	·	·	·	·
6	·	·	·	·	·
5	·	·	·	·	·
4	·	·	·	·	·
3	·	·	·	·	·
2	·	·	·	·	·
1	·	·	·	·	·

(Mark the appropriate number and connect the lines to complete the graph)

On the scale of 1 to 10, project how important you believe this value will be 10 years from now. Chart this number on the graph above.

How has this value changed over the years? Check one of the following.

_____ Upward
_____ Downward
_____ Stable (has not changed much over the years)
_____ Varied upward and downward

List any events that caused this value to either vary upward or downward. If the value remained stable, list the events you think caused it to remain stable.

For what reasons do you maintain this value? That is, how does having this value help you? Describe this in detail below.

How can this value be used directly in Christian service? Describe this below.

List three jobs that will help you use this value.

1.

2.

3.

Value _____

	0 to 10 yrs.	*10 to 15 yrs.*	*15 to 20 yrs.*	*20 to 30 yrs.*	*10 yrs.* +
10	·	·	·	·	·
9	·	·	·	·	·
8	·	·	·	·	·
7	·	·	·	·	·
6	·	·	·	·	·
5	·	·	·	·	·
4	·	·	·	·	·
3	·	·	·	·	·
2	·	·	·	·	·
1	·	·	·	·	·

(Mark the appropriate number and connect the lines to complete the graph)

On the scale of 1 to 10, project how important you believe this value will be 10 years from now. Chart this number on the graph above.

How has this value changed over the years? Check one of the following.

_____ Upward

_____ Downward

_____ Stable (has not changed much over the years)

_____ Varied upward and downward

List any events that caused this value to either vary upward or downward. If the value remained stable, list the events you think caused it to remain stable.

For what reasons do you maintain this value? That is, how does having this value help you? Describe this in detail below.

How can this value be used directly in Christian service? Describe this below.

List three jobs that will help you use this value.

1.

2.

3.

Value _____

	0 to 10 yrs.	10 to 15 yrs.	15 to 20 yrs.	20 to 30 yrs.	10 yrs. +
10	·	·	·	·	·
9	·	·	·	·	·
8	·	·	·	·	·
7	·	·	·	·	·
6	·	·	·	·	·
5	·	·	·	·	·
4	·	·	·	·	·
3	·	·	·	·	·
2	·	·	·	·	·
1	·	·	·	·	·

(Mark the appropriate number and connect the lines to complete the graph)

On the scale of 1 to 10, project how important you believe this value will be 10 years from now. Chart this number on the graph above.

How has this value changed over the years? Check one of the following.

_____ Upward

_____ Downward

_____ Stable (has not changed much over the years)

_____ Varied upward and downward

List any events that caused this value to either vary upward or downward. If the value remained stable, list the events you think caused it to remain stable.

For what reasons do you maintain this value? That is, how does having this value help you? Describe this in detail below.

How can this value be used directly in Christian service? Describe this below.

List three jobs that will help you use this value.

1.

2.

3.

Value _____

	0 to 10 yrs.	10 to 15 yrs.	15 to 20 yrs.	20 to 30 yrs.	10 yrs. +
10	·	·	·	·	·
9	·	·	·	·	·
8	·	·	·	·	·
7	·	·	·	·	·
6	·	·	·	·	·
5	·	·	·	·	·
4	·	·	·	·	·
3	·	·	·	·	·
2	·	·	·	·	·
1	·	·	·	·	·

(Mark the appropriate number and connect the lines to complete the graph)

On the scale of 1 to 10, project how important you believe this value will be 10 years from now. Chart this number on the graph above.

How has this value changed over the years? Check one of the following.

_____ Upward

_____ Downward

_____ Stable (has not changed much over the years)

_____ Varied upward and downward

List any events that caused this value to either vary upward or downward. If the value remained stable, list the events you think caused it to remain stable.

For what reasons do you maintain this value? That is, how does having this value help you? Describe this in detail.

How can this value be used directly in Christian service? Describe this below.

List three jobs that will help you use this value.

1

2.

3.

Value _____

	0 to 10 yrs.	10 to 15 yrs.	15 to 20 yrs.	20 to 30 yrs.	10 yrs +
10	·	·	·	·	·
9	·	·	·	·	·
8	·	·	·	·	·
7	·	·	·	·	·
6	·	·	·	·	·
5	·	·	·	·	·
4	·	·	·	·	·
3	·	·	·	·	·
2	·	·	·	·	·
1	·	·	·	·	·

(Mark the appropriate number and connect the lines to complete the graph)

On the scale of 1 to 10, project how important you believe this value will be 10 years from now. Chart this number on the graph above.

How has this value changed over the years? Check one of the following.

_____ Upward

_____ Downward

_____ Stable (has not changed much over the years)

_____ Varied upward and downward

List any events that caused this value to either vary upward or downward. If the value remained stable, list the events you think caused it to remain stable.

For what reasons do you maintain this value? That is, how does having this value help you? Describe this in detail below.

How can this value be used directly in Christian service? Describe this below.

List three jobs that will help you use this value.

1.

2.

3.

4
Where Am I Going?

We have taken time to look at who you are and what is important to you. Now let's ask the next question, "Where am I going?" David Clark has written a book entitled *If You Don't Know Where You Are Going, You Probably Will End Up Some Place Else.* Many people launch their careers by looking for a job and taking the first one that is offered. That is great if your only concern is having a job. But we feel that you have interests, abilities, and dreams that are leading you. In the back of your mind there are things you want to accomplish. Those dreams may relate to success, respect, wealth, marriage and family, adventure, or travel. Whatever it is, you have a dream. Those things don't just happen; they must be planned for. In fact, some of the greatest joys in life are found in working toward a dream. This chapter will help you take those dreams and translate them into some realistic and attainable goals. When you have defined those goals, then you can look at the career that will most likely help you in attaining those goals.

Human beings are goal-oriented by nature. When you have a clear goal, you are able to direct your efforts with maximum effectiveness. Having goals keeps us from spending a lot of time and energy in activities that will not lead us to any substantial achievement. Goals also keep us from worrying about things that are unimportant.

Goals are essential to good mental health. Without them you will probably lose much of your meaning in life. Furthermore, you will fail to develop your full potential without goals. When you have goals, the natural result is that you will strive for greater and greater accomplishments. Therefore, your meaning and purpose and general mental well-being will be enhanced.

The Bible does not deal with goals directly. The Bible talks about goals in an indirect manner. But there are some spiritual truths that you need to be aware of.

In the Sermon on the Mount we find some examples of the kinds of goals we should strive for as Christians. Our Lord said, "Do not lay up for yourselves treasures upon earth" (Matt. 6:19, NASB). He is pointing out that goals which relate to physical, material, and financial stability are not as important as goals relating to spiritual maturity, growth, and development. The emphasis in this passage is not that physical considerations are unimportant, but that God will take care of those needs if you will concern yourself with matters relating to his kingdom.

We should consider the way goals have influenced certain lives. It has been said that Jesus' life was lived with the shadow of the cross penetrating his entire ministry. The cross and man's need for salvation kept Jesus from yielding to temptation in the wilderness. It led him in training his disciples. It even led Jesus to Jerusalem the week he was crucified. Later in the life of Paul we see a man who had in mind exactly what he wanted to accomplish. He wanted to tell the world about Jesus Christ. For that reason, he traveled throughout Asia Minor and Greece establishing churches. He wanted to go to Rome and preach; when he was arrested he appealed to Caesar thus forcing the Roman authorities to send him to Rome.

One last example of goal direction is seen in Acts 1:8. "And you shall be My witnesses both in Jerusalem, and in all Judea and Samaria, and even to the remotest part of the earth" (NASB).

Kinds of Goals

There are many kinds of goals, but for our purpose we have divided goals into four classifications: health goals, spiritual goals, career goals, and personal goals. Each of these goals is intertwining and interdependent. It is impossible to completely separate one goal from the other because individuals must have overlapping goals in each of these four areas in order to feel a sense of continuity and completeness. Having goals in only one area will tend to produce an overbalance causing a person to become fragmented in his efforts to fulfill his potential.

Spiritual Goals

Why do you need to set spiritual goals for yourself? There are several reasons. First, many Christians tend to become stagnant in their spiritual lives. They make an initial commitment to Christ but then they get busy in other areas of their lives and their spiritual life degenerates to attending church on Sunday and nothing else. Second, a Christian is not perfect. Growth and development need to take place. Paul refers to the Corinthian Christians as spiritual babes because they have not grown. Third, our daily life can become monotonous and boring without spiritual goals to keep you reaching ahead. Fourth, God wants to use you as part of his kingdom to supply the needs of the world.

There are certain areas in which every Christian should establish some spiritual goals. Every Christian needs to have goals that relate to personal spiritual growth. This area relates to the Christian's knowledge and understanding of the Scriptures and to the Christian's prayer life. Some appropriate goals in this area could be to establish a period for personal worship on a daily basis, to read the Bible through, to complete a Bible study on a particular book or subject, or to read some books on prayer and to develop a list of prayer concerns. The important thing is to determine where you are spiritually and where you want to be, then establish some goals that will lead you along that journey.

Another area for spiritual goals is in terms of ministry to others. This includes evangelism, helping others in need, or being a teacher to help others know more about themselves and the Lord. D. L. Moody, one of the great evangelists of the 1800's, had a goal of personally sharing Christ with at least one person every day. You may want to establish a similar goal. Or you may want to learn how to witness to someone. In terms of ministry to others, you may know areas, such as in local hospitals, where you can be a volunteer. You could make it your goal to help some person financially or in some other way.

An important area for spiritual goals relates to the church. The church depends upon its people for growth, for ministry. The first goal for every Christian should be to define and develop his talent that will benefit the church. A good goal can be to find the area where you can be of service to the church and to get involved in that service. Of course every member should be involved in reaching out to bring others into the fellowship of the church.

The final area for spiritual goals relates to fulfilling life's calling. God has called us to faith, and now he has called us to be involved in the world as his people. He has called us to his service. Our goal in this area should be to determine our special calling and to carry out that calling.

The results will be more than evident. Rather than your spiritual life being stagnant, it will be dynamic. You will see yourself growing, being excited and interested in life. There will be the blessing of Christ when you hear him say, "Well done, thou good and faithful servant."

Health Goals

A person who is not physically fit will not be a fully productive person in life or in a career. When a person has an illness, he usually makes an immediate appointment to see a doctor. The doctor then makes a diagnosis and prescribes some sort of treatment. In effect, the doctor is remedying an illness.

Health goals are designed to prevent a person from getting ill. Health goals are *preventive* instead of *remedial.* Obviously, all of us are going to get ill at some time in our lives. However, a well-developed set of health goals may prevent many illnesses in addition to helping us perform at a higher peak of efficiency. A set of health goals should include a program of exercise, proper diet, ongoing medical care, and the ability to manage stress.

For the body to perform efficiently, the cardiovascular system must be able to function maximally, and the muscular system must be able to handle the physical demands placed upon the body. Daily exercise, a plan of action, can help the cardiovascular system supply the body with the necessary materials to perform at a high level. When the cardiovascular system and muscular system are fully functioning, the energy levels actually increase significantly, enabling you to increase your productivity on the job. Good goals in this area would be to find a recreational sport within the community in which to participate or to start an individual program of physical conditioning.

It goes without saying that a proper diet will help you maintain proper weight control and will increase your resistance to illness. Many young people fail to see the significance of developing good eating habits. You should seriously examine the kinds of things you regularly eat and the amount you eat because you may be building eating habits which ten to fifteen years from now could cause you to become overweight or a good candidate for heart problems and chronic illness. People who are chronically overweight miss more work and are less productive than people who maintain a proper body weight. Thus, you should keep in mind when developing health goals that diet and weight control are extremely important.

Most of us go to a doctor only when we are ill. However, the person who is developing good health goals will know that it is wise to get regular physical exams in order to monitor any potential physical illnesses. You should not avoid writing a health goal in this area.

How you learn to manage stress is becoming an increasingly important health goal in our modern world. Stress-related illnesses cause a significant number of people to lose time from the job in addition to making them malfunction while at work. A person who is unable to handle stress will pay a high price. Some doctors believe that prolonged stress can lead to migraine headaches, ulcers, heart irregularity, and mental illness. Some general signs of stress overload are irritability, insomnia, fatigue, weight change, intestinal disturbances, and respiratory problems. Psychologically, stress can cause high levels of anxiety—that worried, "uptight" feeling that something bad or unpleasant is going to happen even if there is no real threat. This can lead to nervousness, trembling, dizziness, pounding heart, inability to slow down or relax, abnormal blood pressure, and on and on. Another extreme reaction to stress overload is the depression that leads to apathy and withdrawal.

As you can see, developing ways to effectively manage stress can become critical in your career development. You should definitely write goals in the area of stress management. A good first goal, for example, may be to do a self-analysis of how well you currently manage stress. You may also want to look at the kinds of stress that seem to interfere with your full productivity and at the kinds of jobs that would bring on this kind of stress.

The first area, therefore, in which you must write goals is health. We hope we have sufficiently explained the importance of preventative health goals in career development. Most people in their career planning leave this important area out and, therefore, fail to consider one of the most important aspects of career success.

Personal Goals

It has been said that individuals are basically selfish in their motivation. They look out for themselves first and others second. We don't buy this. Granted, there may be many people in this world who are selfish, but we believe that most individuals when given the chance will consider others as well as themselves. Thus, in developing personal goals we believe you will not be selfishly motivated. Nevertheless, you need to set some goals that are only personally important to you. You need to look at some things that are only important to you and decide if you really want to accomplish them. For example, you may be a jogger. Your personal goal will simply be to be able to jog a certain distance so many times per week. You may want to travel to a foreign country someday as a long-range goal. The kind of house you hope to own someday may be a personal goal.

Career Goals

We have already been emphasizing the importance of developing career goals. At this point, we should stress that career goals need to be in harmony with other goals. That is, they must not interfere with the accomplishment of other goals.

A career is more than just going to work each morning. A career is a series of roles which a person plays. The nature of this role has an impact on all other goals. When a career is in harmony with your other goals, you have markedly increased your chances of developing your full potential.

Setting Goals

Setting goals is not an easy task. Goals must be something that you want to accomplish, not goals set entirely by others. You must have a commitment to your goals and must fully understand your reasons for these goals. If you don't, you will find ways not to accomplish them, ways to avoid disciplining yourself to do the things necessary to accomplish them, and ways to short-circuit your achievements. You may not do this consciously, however. If you have goals that you do not feel are important, you will have great difficulty in motivating yourself. If you have goals that you really want to accomplish, motivation becomes only a side issue instead of a paramount issue.

Here are some guidelines to follow in setting goals.

1. *A goal must be attainable.* You should not set goals which

are totally unrealistic or can never be achieved. Some people who are failure-oriented will set goals that are too high so they can fail. This, in turn, reinforces their failure syndrome.

To make this more difficult, you will probably have to set many of your goals without sufficient data. Since you cannot predict the future all of the time, you must make successive educated guesses. Finding a balance between what is realistic and what cannot be accomplished is extremely difficult. If you set your goals too low, you will fail to reach your full potential. When the potential in you is not developed, you may suffer the anxieties of wasting your life. On the other side of the coin, if you set your goals too high you are guaranteed failure.

2. *A goal must serve to strengthen you as a person.* William Glasser, a prominent psychiatrist, points out that our society has many people who are negatively addicted. They become addicted to drugs, to alcohol, to overeating, to poor management of their physical health, and so on. Negative addictions tear you down and prevent you from becoming the person you want to become. The successful person, according to Glasser, is positively addicted. He is committed or addicted to things which strengthen him and develop his potential. If you have a goal, you should determine if the goal will strengthen you as a person.

3. *A goal must be specific.* Look at the following example of a career goal.

"I will have a good job in four years." This goal is not specific. In fact, this may be many goals in one. The person has not spelled out what a good job would be. Things such as location, kind of work, money, working hours, and so forth, were left out. To make this goal more specific look at the following one:

"I will become an accountant after completion of four years of college in my hometown." This goal is more specific although it still could be made more specific.

4. *A goal should have a time frame.* You need to know when you plan to ultimately accomplish a goal. In goal three this person said the goal would be accomplished in four years. Any goal should have a definite time limitation.

5. *A goal should be flexible.* You must be able to adjust or change your goal. Do not lock yourself into a goal. Keep an open mind. The person in the example who wants to be an accountant could possibly change his mind if he happens to find a career he believes will be more rewarding.

6. *A goal must be something that you personally want to accomplish.* We keep emphasizing this because we feel that it is often difficult to distinguish our goals from the goals of others. We see people on television or read about people in the newspaper who have certain goals, and we believe they may be best for us. In reality, the goals would not. Furthermore, people around us often give us advice about goals; we have to be careful to determine if these are goals that only others want for us or are these goals we want. Don't rule out advice from others because advice from others can be very helpful. However, remember that you are ultimately responsible for your goals and will eventually have to accomplish them yourself.

7. *A goal must have some sort of payoff.* A goal must have a reward for you. B. F. Skinner pointed out that anytime a behavior is rewarded it tends to be repeated. If your goals do not have a clear-cut reward in it for you, you will have difficulty in achieving future goals. Don't overlook the importance of the payoff in goals.

A goal is something to be accomplished at a future time. It should meet the guidelines we've just mentioned. The things you do to get to goals are called *objectives.* If you want to become an engineer after four years of college, there are literally hundreds of objectives that must be accomplished. Organizing all of your objectives into some sort of pattern is called a *strategy.* Strategies are like football game plans. They're similar to a plan of attack. If you know your goal is to become an engineer, then you must begin to plan your strategy to accomplish this goal.

Objectives are not always worked out entirely before you start pursuing a goal. Objectives may be both long- and short-range, daily, weekly, or yearly.

Review

It is important to set goals that you can accomplish. Your personal development and mental well-being depends upon your ability to set and achieve goals. Goals should be written in four areas—health goals, spiritual goals, personal goals, and career goals. Goals should follow certain guidelines which we listed. Once you establish a goal, you must develop objectives to accomplish the goal. A series of objectives to accomplish a goal is called a strategy. Objectives and strategies can be developed on a long- and short-range basis.

We are now ready to take you through a series of exercises designed to help you set some goals. Below list ten things you would like to accomplish in your lifetime. Do not stop until you have listed them. This may take some time and thought.

Goal   Rank

1.

2.

3.

4.

5.

6.

7.

8.

9.

· 10.

Now go back and rank these goals in order of importance on the right-hand side of the page. Rewrite the five most important goals below in order of importance. Beside each goal is a place to check the seven guidelines for goals that we have told you about. Check each guideline that this goal meets. If it meets all seven guidelines, it is a well-written goal.

Goal Area	Goal	Guideline Met
	1.	1 2 3 4 5 6 7
	2.	1 2 3 4 5 6 7
	3.	1 2 3 4 5 6 7
	4.	1 2 3 4 5 6 7
	5.	1 2 3 4 5 6 7

To the left of each goal write which of the four goal areas the goal will fall into: health goal, spiritual goal, personal goal, or career goal.

You will probably have many more goals than this in your lifetime. We are going to ask you to write some more goals in the specific goal areas that we have discussed. Under each goal area we want you to write three goals.

Health Goals	Guidelines Met
1.	1 2 3 4 5 6 7
2.	1 2 3 4 5 6 7
3.	1 2 3 4 5 6 7

Spiritual Goals

1.   1 2 3 4 5 6 7

2.   1 2 3 4 5 6 7

3.   1 2 3 4 5 6 7

Personal Goals

1.   1 2 3 4 5 6 7

2.   1 2 3 4 5 6 7

3.   1 2 3 4 5 6 7

Career Goals

1.   1 2 3 4 5 6 7

2.   1 2 3 4 5 6 7

3.   1 2 3 4 5 6 7

You have probably written a long list of goals by now. Are they really goals that you want to accomplish? Let's see if we can help you answer that question. Below is a list of times for one day. In each time frame list anything you did yesterday to help you accomplish any of your goals.

8:00-9:00

9:00-10:00

10:00-11:00

11:00-12:00

12:00-1:00

1:00-2:00

2:00-3:00

3:00-4:00

4:00-5:00

5:00-6:00

6:00-7:00

7:00-8:00

8:00-9:00

9:00-10:00

10:00-11:00

Did you do anything to accomplish your goals yesterday? Which goals did you work on the most? Which goals did you not work on at all? Do you still want to accomplish all of these goals? These are some questions that will help you briefly assess the goals you have already listed. We are now going to help you pull these goals together into an accompanying strategy for each one. Look again at all the goals you've written. We want you to write one major goal from each of the four goal areas. You do not have to write a goal that you've already written unless you want it to be the one major goal.

Health Goal:

_____

_____

Look at your top five values from chapter 3. Which of these values would be met by this goal? Write them below.

1.
2.
3.
4.
5.

Rank the importance of this goal to yourself on the following scale. Circle one.

Little Importance   Very Important
1   2   3   4   5   6   7   8   9   10

Write as many specific objectives that you can think of to accomplish your goal.

1.

2.

3.

4.

5.

6.

7.

8.

9.

10

11

12

13

14

15

16

17

18

19.

20.

Circle the number of the objectives you are going to complete in the next six months.

Spiritual Goal: _____

_____

Look at your top five values from chapter 3. Which of these values would be met by this goal? Write them below.

1

2.

3.

4.

5.

Rank the importance of this goal to yourself on the following scale. Circle one.

Little Importance   Very Important
1   2   3   4   5   6   7   8   9   10

Write as many specific objectives that you can think of to accomplish your goal.

1.

2.

3.

4.

5.

6.

7.

8.

9.

10.

11.

12.

13.

14.

15.

16.

17.

·18.

19.

20.

Circle the number of the objectives you are going to complete in the next six months.

Career Goal: _____

_____

Look at your top five values from chapter 3. Which of these values would be met by this goal? Write them below.

1

2.

3.

4.

5.

Rank the importance of this goal to yourself on the following scale. Circle one.

Little Importance   Very Important
1   2   3   4   5   6   7   8   9   10

Write as many specific objectives that you can think of to accomplish your goal.

1.

2.

3.

4.

5.

6.

7.

8.

9.

10.

11.

12.

13.

14.

15.

16.

17.

18.

19.

20.

Circle the number of the objectives you are going to complete in the next six months.

Personal Goal: _____

_____

Look at your top five values from chapter 3. Which of these values would be met by this goal? Write them below.

1.

2.

3.

4.

5.

Rank the importance of this goal to yourself on the following scale. Circle one.

Little Importance   Very Important

1   2   3   4   5   6   7   8   9   10

Write as many specific objectives that you can think of to accomplish your goal.

1.

2.

3.

4.

5.

6.

7.

8.

9.

10.

11.

12.

13.

14.

15.

16.

17.

18.

19.

20.

Circle the number of the objectives you are going to complete in the next six months.

5
How Do I Choose an Occupation?

If you are going to select a career where you can develop your full potential, you must be able to integrate several things. You must be skilled at matching your abilities, values, and goals to an ongoing career. You must also be able to match your major way of contacting others—communication style and interpersonal relationships—to a specific career. Up to this point we have looked at these areas extensively. In this chapter we are going to help you make an analysis of five careers. We will also show you a matching process whereby you will be able to match your values, abilities, goals, interpersonal preferences, and communication functions to jobs.

We are using the term *career* to denote your entire work life from entry to retirement. You should make every effort to see the whole picture when studying a career. The terms *job* and *occupation* are used synonymously. This is the specific kind of work you are performing whereas a career is the whole series of jobs or occupations that you will occupy in a lifetime.

Before we begin the matching process, let's review some of the more important aspects of career exploration.

1. *Career choice is a changing lifelong process.* You are now and will continue to make career choices for the rest of your life. Whether consciously or unconsciously, career choices are constantly being made.

2. *Career choice requires both extensive and intensive exploration.* Career choice is very hard work. Those who avoid it or put it off are almost certain to doom themselves to underem-

ployment, that is, to a job which will not fully utilize their potential.

3. *Most people will change occupations several times in a lifetime.* Some sources say that people under thirty-five years of age change jobs on the average of once every eighteen months and over thirty-five years of age, once every four years. We change and therefore we seek new and differing career experiences.

4. *Career choice involves matching abilities, values, goals, communication style and interpersonal preferences to specific jobs.*

5. *Job satisfaction and success is dependent on having the kind of career which best utilizes the above factors.*

6. *People are multi-potential.* People can perform and be happy in many different kinds of occupations. There is no one best job for you.

7. *The kind of career you choose will determine the kind of role you will play as a Christian.*

8. *Career choice is a series of choices—not just one choice.* Career choice is a long series of choices strung out over your entire life, beginning at birth.

9. *The development of good mental health is dependent upon having an occupation where you are successful.* In his study Abraham Maslow found that the one essential ingredient in the development of high levels of good mental health was the commitment to a job that one feels to be important. He found that almost without exception highly healthy people had a job they thought was important and that they were committed to. In fact, he discovered that these healthy people often had difficulty distinguishing between work and play. Their job was enjoyable, and they did not perceive it as work.

Religious Vs. Secular Work

Many young people who are active in their church program or in a campus ministry group are struggling with the question, "Should I go into full-time religious work?" There are many reasons why you would want to consider the possibility of full-time religious work. Perhaps the primary reason comes from a deep spiritual commitment on your part. You are a committed Christian who is studying the Bible and growing in understanding of the Christian life. You feel a great deal of fulfillment from your Christian life-style and you want to make sure that this sense of fulfillment continues. There may be a pastor or a youth minister who has provided you with an excellent example which you want to follow. There is the desire to lead others in experiencing and understanding the same kind of spiritual commitment you have experienced. The natural result is to make a commitment to the full-time ministry.

Many people enter the full-time ministry as an environmental preference over working in the secular world. A religious vocation usually means being surrounded by Christian people who understand your commitment to Christianity. There is neither struggle with the secular world in terms of moral or ethical standards nor the struggle of living as a Christian among those who do not understand your commitment. If this is your motivation to enter a religious occupation, you should analyze carefully this motivation to be certain that it is not a withdrawal from involvement in the world. Christians are called to service in the world. Even the full-time ministry involves work in the world. Jesus spent most of his time working with people who were called "publicans and sinners" and was criticized for it.

Some enter the full-time ministry for the prestige that comes with it. Americans respect the clergy. People who are church members tend to look to ministers for guidance and hold them in high esteem. Being in the full-time ministry is viewed as a deeper level of commitment by other Christians. While it is important that you feel good about what you are doing, you must be careful that this is not the only reason for entering full-time religious work.

The decision about entering full-time religious work is a

difficult one at best. It is very personal. It grows out of your own relationship to God. Because of this, it is often difficult to know when you are responding from your own desires and when you are deciding as a result of God's leadership. Biblical material relating to God's calling can give us some insight into this issue.

In the Scriptures we find evidence of a divine call of God to special religious responsibilities. Abraham, Moses, Isaiah, Matthew, Peter, and James are a few examples. They each came to a point in their lives in which they experienced a call to a special responsibility. Each was given a command by God to carry out a task. Abraham was called to go to a place called Canaan and be the father of a nation. Moses was called to lead the Hebrews from Egyptian slavery. Isaiah was called to be a spokesman for God. Matthew, Peter, and James were called to become followers of Jesus by being disciples.

These callings did not come as an isolated event. There were many events and circumstances that led up to each calling. Abraham was in the process of migrating away from Ur of the Chaldeas when his father died in Haran. It was then that God called him to move further. Isaiah was praying in the temple not long after King Uzziah died. There was political and spiritual turmoil when God called him to be a prophet. Similar critical situations were found in the lives of Peter and Matthew and especially in the life of Paul. Thus, you can see that in most cases, the call to religious work is not an isolated event, but a part of a person's total growth and maturing process.

All of these men knew they were being called to special religious work. There was no question about it. They did not say, "I think God is calling me." However, not everyone was ready to say yes to the call of God. Moses is an example of one who did not want to follow God's leadership. God was persistent and dealt with Moses until he agreed to follow him. In short, if God is calling you to some special work, then he will continue to do so until you respond. If you definitely sense God is calling you to special religious work, by all means follow this calling with all your energy and effort. On the other hand, if there is not a definite sense of calling, you should consider the secular world for work in addition to analyzing how you will integrate your Christian commitment with a nonreligious occupation. Remember that lay persons are a vital part of the church. They are the ones who go into the everyday world and present God's teachings.

There are many ways the Christian lay person can be involved in Christian work as an avocation. You can serve as a volunteer youth worker or musician, even pastor a small church that cannot afford a full-time minister. There are available for volunteers more and more short-term mission projects that last from two weeks up to two years. In these projects you can work side by side with regular missionaries in foreign countries and in other areas in the United States where few churches exist. The greatest need today is for laypeople who will move to a new area and voluntarily serve as church staff members. Paul is the primary example in the Bible of one who served on a voluntary basis while earning a living at another profession. He did not accept money from the churches he worked with but volunteered his services while working as a tentmaker.

Finding God's will as a full-time religious worker or in the secular world of work requires continuous effort. In his book *The Will of God,* Leslie Weatherhead, a British pastor, gives several suggestions for determining God's will for your life. Weatherhead suggests that you use common sense first. He contends that God does not ask you to do something irrational nor does he ask you to do something that does not make sense. He advises that you consult great literature, particularly biographies. See how God has dealt with and led these great men of faith. God may deal with you in similar ways.

You may get advice from a friend. Many times you are so involved in making the decision that you cannot see things objectively. A good friend can help you by being honest with you and by helping you clarify the issues that are involved in making the decision. You may also talk with those already in religious occupations to determine how they resolved their career choice.

It is also a good idea to listen to the voice of the church. The church speaks to the people about needs that surround it. It may speak about the need to witness, service, missions, or the material requirements evident in church. God speaks through his messenger in the preaching ministry and through the collective gathering of a congregation. A last suggestion is to look at circumstances. Many times God will use circumstances to give you direction.

When you consider all these suggestions, you must ultimately decide on which direction to take. You must follow your own inner leadership. When confirmed by friends, the voice of the church, other religious leaders, and your various life circumstances, you can be confident that God is leading you in finding his will for your life. Romans 8:28 best describes this final decision to act on either a religious ministry or secular career. "And we know that God causes all things to work together for good to those who love God, to those who are called according to His purpose" (NASB).

What Do I Need To Know About an Occupation?

Obviously there are many things one needs to know about an occupation in order to determine if this is an occupation which will help them develop their individual potential. We suggest the following things as absolutely essential.

1. *Kind of work.* You must know exactly what a person does on the job. You need to know the kinds of decisions they have to make, working hours, the kinds of stresses, and so forth.

2. *Career patterns.* Although very little is written about career patterns, this is perhaps one of the most important aspects of all career information. A career pattern is the pattern that people characteristically follow once they enter a particular

job. For example, entry level jobs are those jobs which require the minimum amount of education and experience to enter. Once a person enters this job they progress in some direction. Twenty years later they may wind up as a company president. The jobs they held while progressing to the presidency make up their career pattern. The way to determine career patterns is to look at the number people entering a particular job, the outlook for the future of this job, and the top position attained by persons who held this entry level job.

3. *Where people are employed.* Where you live and work, geographically, will always be an important part of your career. However, you must also know what companies or organizations employ the people in the kind of job you have chosen.

4. *Qualifications.* Most skilled jobs require training. Some require extensive training before entry while others are essentially on-the-job training. In our highly sophisticated technological work environment, more and more jobs are requiring more and more training before entry. You must be aware of the training and educational requirements at an early date so you may plan accordingly.

5. *Employment outlook.* What are the trends for your chosen occupation? Is there a demand for this kind of work? Is this kind of work seasonal?

6. *Earnings and working conditions.* You must have some idea of the kind of money you will make in a chosen occupation. Although many people downplay the importance of money when choosing an occupation, it is still one of the most important factors in career choice. If you do not make enough money to live comfortably, or your job does not hold hope for making enough money, you will not be able to grow and progress at an effective rate. Maslow, in his studies, said that we all have needs. These needs line up in order of importance and as the top needs are met we move on to the others. We must first meet our first need for food, clothing, and shelter and all other needs will have to, for the most part, wait. Once the basic needs are met we are able to move on to other needs which

are more concerned with achievement and fulfillment of our potential.

7. *Related jobs.* All jobs have other jobs which are related. You need to know some of the jobs that are similar or at least require similar skills.

Where Do I Find Out Information About Occupations?

Occupational information abounds almost everywhere. We see it in the newspapers, on television, on billboards, and so on. Filtering through to find out what we want to know about a particular occupation is sometimes difficult. Companies and organizations often develop elaborate career materials about occupations within their company. These materials can be very informative. They should be viewed carefully and with caution, however. While companies and organizations are interested in providing job information, they are also interested in advertising for good employees. Their material may be slated more on the optimistic side. Nevertheless, do not fail to use these sources. You can obtain many helpful tips about jobs by writing companies and organizations.

Talking with people who are already working in a particular occupation is often helpful. You can easily determine what they do, what they like or dislike about a job, and some of the career patterns involved. Sometimes by simply making an appointment with an official of a company, such as a personnel director, you can find a great deal of information about an occupation.

The library is perhaps one of the best sources of occupational information. We suggest the following sources of information.

Occupational Outlook Handbook. This is an excellent source of updated information. This book is published by the United States Department of Labor Bureau of Statistics and is updated yearly.

Dictionary of Occupational Titles. This book is also published by the United States Government. It contains information on over forty thousand jobs.

Career Biographies
SRA Monographs
Career Monographs

Career information in the printed form often gets outdated quickly. Be very careful in reading this information in order to know when the material was written.

Selecting Careers for Study

We are now ready to help you begin selecting occupations for indepth study. We will first help you think of a long list of potential occupations. We will show you how to match these jobs with your values, abilities, goals, communication functions, and interpersonal relationships.

If you could have any ten jobs, what would they be? That is, if you had an ideal job and could have your pick, which ten ideal jobs would you pick? List them below.

1.
2.
3.
4.
5.
6.
7.
8.
9.
10.

Think of three people who seem to have an exciting job and seem to be very happy. List their jobs below.

1.
2.
3.

Look at the classified-ad section of your local newspaper. Read over all the jobs that are advertised. Pick five that seem interesting to you. List them below.

1.
2.

3.

4.

5.

Look at the list of jobs on the following pages. Pick ten jobs that seem interesting to you that you have not already listed. List them below.

1.

2.

3.

4.

5.

6.

7.

8.

9.

10.

Ask three friends what they see as the ideal job for you. List those jobs below.

1.

2.

3.

Think of some places that you have been over the past several months which brought you into contact with someone who had an unusual and apparently exciting job. List three of these jobs.

1.

2.

3.

You now have a list of thirty-four jobs. You may know very little about each one of them because you have not had the opportunity to thoroughly explore them. Next we want you to look at the sources of information that we previously suggested and list ten more jobs that seem interesting (information from employers, people you know, and from the library).

1.

2.

3.
4.
5.
6.
7.
8.
9.
10.

Occupational List *

Foundry Occupations
  Patternmakers
  Molders
  Coremakers
Machining Occupations
  All-round Machinists
  Instrument Makers (Mechanical)
    Machine Tool Operators
  Set-up Workers (Machine Tools)
  Tool and Die Makers
Printing Occupations
  Bookbinders and Related Workers
  Composing Room Occupations
  Electrotypers and Stereotypers
  Lithographic Occupations
  Photoengravers
  Printing Press Operators
Automobile Painters

Blacksmiths
Blue-collar Supervisors
Boilermaking Occupations
Boiler Tenders
Electroplaters
Forge Shop Occupations
Furniture Upholsterers
Millwrights
Motion Picture Projectionists
Photographic Laboratory Worker
Stationary Engineers
Welders
Bookkeeping Worker
Cashier
Postal Clerk
Secretary and Stenographer
Computer Programmer
Systems Analyst
Bank Officer
Bank Teller
Actuary
Underwriter

* Most of these occupations were taken from the *Occupational Outlook Handbook.*

Accountant
Advertising Worker
Buyer
City Manager
Credit Manager
Hotel Manager
Industrial Traffic Manager
Lawyer
Marketing Research Worker
Personnel and Labor Relations Worker
Public Relations Worker
Purchasing Agent
Urban Planner
Pest Controller
Cooks and Chefs
Barber
Cosmetologists
Funeral Director & Embalmer
FBI Special Agent
Firefighter
Police Officer
State Police Officer
Government Construction Inspector
Government Health and Regulatory Inspector
Occupational Safety and Health Worker
Mail Carrier
Kindergarten and Elementary School Teacher
Secondary School Teacher
College and University Teacher

Librarian
Automobile Salesworker
Insurance Agent and Broker
Manufacturers' Salesworker
Models
Real Estate Salesworker and Broker
Retail Trade Salesworker
Securities Salesworker
Wholesale Trade Salesworker
Asbestos and Insulation Worker
Bricklayer and Stonemason
Carpenter
Construction Laborer
Electrician (Construction)
Floor Covering Installer
Glaziers
Lathers
Marble Setters, Tile Setters, & Terrazzo Worker
Operating Engineer (Construction machinery operator)
Painter and Paperhanger
Plasterer
Plumber and Pipefitter
Roofer
Sheet-Metal Worker
Air Traffic Controller
Airplane Mechanic
Airplane Pilot
Flight Attendant
Reservation, Ticket, and Passenger Agent
Merchant Marine Officer

Merchant Marine Sailor
Railroad Brake Operator
Railroad Conductor
Locomotive Engineer
Railroad Telegrapher, Telephoner and Tower Operator
Intercity Busdriver
Local Truckdrivers
Long Distance Truckdrivers
Taxicab Drivers
Foresters
Forestry Technicians
Range Manager
Soil Conservationist
Aerospace Engineer
Agricultural Engineer
Biomedical Engineer
Ceramic Engineer
Chemical Engineer
Civil Engineer
Electrical Engineer
Industrial Engineer
Mechanical Engineer
Metallurgical Engineer
Mining Engineer
Petroleum Engineer
Geologist
Geophysist
Meteorologist
Oceanographer
Biochemist
Life Scientist
Social Scientist
Mathematician
Statistician
Astronomer
Chemist
Physicist
Drafter
Engineering and Science Technician
Surveyor
Air-Conditioning, Refrigeration, & Heating Mechanics
Appliance Repairer
Automobile Body Repairers
Automobile Mechanics
Boat-Motor Mechanics
Computer Service Technician
Diesel Mechanics
Jewelers
Locksmiths
Piano and Organ Tuner and Repairer
Shoe Repairer
Television and Radio Service Technician
Truck Mechanic and Bus Mechanic
Watch Repairer
Dentist
Dental Assistant
Dental Hygienist
Dental Laboratory Technician
Chiropractors
Optometrist
Osteopathic Physician
Physician
Podiatrist
Veterinarian

Electrocardiograph Technician
Medical Assistant
Medical Laboratory Worker
Operating Room Technician
Radiologic (X-Ray) Technologist
Respiratory Therapy Worker
Registered Nurse (RN)
Licensed Vocational Nurse
Occupational Therapist
Physical Therapist
Speech Pathologist and Audiologist
Dietitians
Health Services Administrator
Pharmacist
Anthropologist
Economist
Geographer
Historian
Political Scientist
Psychologist
Sociologist
School Counselor
Employment Counselor
Rehabilitation Counselor
Protestant Minister
Rabbi
Roman Catholic Priest
Home Economist
Recreation Worker
Social Worker
Actor
Actress

Dancer
Musician
Singer
Architects
Commercial Artist
Industrial Designers
Interior Designers
Landscape Architects
Photographer
Newspaper Reporter
Interpreter
Manufacturing
  Advertising Layout Artist
  Aerospace Technician
  Architectural Draftsman
  Bookkeeper
  Building Inspector
  Electronic Technician
  Environmental Health Technician
  Furniture Upholsterer
  Personnel Interviewer
  Purchasing Agent
  Technical Illustrator
Public Service
  Animal Keeper
  Physical Therapy Assistant
  Bank Teller
  Child Day Care Worker
  Court Reporter
  Fishing Culture Technician
  Highway Patrolman
  Horticulturist Technician
  Keypunch Operator
  Legal Secretary

Medical Laboratory Assistant
Mail Carrier
Medical Secretary
Nuclear Medical Technician
Offset Press Operator
PBX Operator
Receptionist
Recreation Leader
Soil Conservationist
Stenographer
Teacher's Aide
Marine Science
Chemical Laboratory Technician
Data Processing Machine Operator
Game Warden
Diesel Mechanic
Pest Control Operator
Personal Services
Airline Ticket Agent
Ambulance Driver
Barber
Cabinetmaker
Dietetic Technician
Floral Designer
Inhalation Therapist
Locksmith
Model
Motel Manager
Painter
Photographer
Restaurant Manager
Theater Manager
Watch Repairman
Transportation
Accounting Clerk
Aircraft Mechanic
Airline Stewardess
Automobile Body Repairman
Diesel Mechanic
Motorcycle Mechanic
Travel Agent
Construction
Architectural Draftsman
Building Inspector
Cement Mason
Civil Engineering Technician
Elevator Construction
Landscape Gardener
Plasterer
Plumbing Inspector
Roofer
Sandblaster
Structural Ironworker
Communications and Media
Advertising Layout Artist
Copy Reader
Copy Writer
Dark Room Technician
Data Processing Machine Operator
Data Processing Machine Serviceman
Electronics Technician
Lithographic Cameraman
Lithographic Offset Pressman

Motion Picture Projectionist
Photojournalist
Radio-Television Announcer
Sign Painter
Television Cameraman
Environment
Biomedical Technician
Chemical Laboratory Technician
Environmental Health Technician
Fish Culture Technician
Food Production Technician
Horticulture Technician
Meteorologist Technician
Oceanographer
Pest Control Operator
Soil Conservationist
Fine Arts and Humanities
Floral Designer
Interior Decorator
Musical Instrument Repairman
Ornamental Ironworker
Photoengraver
Piano Technician
Health
Contact Lens Technician
Dental Assistant
Dental Laboratory Technician

Dietetic Technician
Electrocardiograph Technician
Histologic Technician
Medical Assistant
Medical Secretary
Medical Technologist
Optometric Assistant
Physical Therapy Assistant
Physician Assistant
Surgical Technician
Agri-Business and Natural Resources
Dairy Farmer
Farm and Garden Salesperson
Forestry Aid
Park Ranger Assistant
Marketing and Distribution
Automobile Salesman
Bakery Routeman
Chain Store Manager
Credit Manager
Displayman
Finance Company Manager
Industrial Truck Operator
Junior Accountant
Pharmacy Helper
Purchasing Agent
Retail Buyer
Telephone Service Representative
Teletype Operator
Vending Routeman

Look at the list of religious jobs. Pick the five that seem most interesting to you and list them below.

1.
2.
3.
4.
5.

Church Ministry
  Pastor
  Assistant Pastor
  Education Director
  Music Director
  Youth Director
  Children's Director
  Evangelism Minister
  Recreation Director
Education
  College President
  College Professor
  Seminary Professor
  College Administrators
  Seminary Administrators
  Christian School Principal
  Christian School Teacher
  Day Care Director
  Day Care Worker
Communications
  Newspaper Editor
  Reporter
  Photographer
  Radio Announcer
  Television Programming
  Printers

  Military Chaplain
  Prison Chaplain
  Industrial Chaplain
  Christian Social Worker
Denominational Service
  Administrators
  Program Consultants:
    Missions
    Church Administration
    Christian Education
    Evangelism
    Christian Life
    Stewardship
  Campus Minister
  Evangelists
Medicine
  Hospital Administrator
  Dietician
  Doctors
  Nurses
Clerical
  Secretaries
  Receptionists
Missions
  Evangelists
  Pastors
  School Administrators
  Teachers

Services   Hospital Administrators
  Pastoral Counselor   Seminary Professors
  Hospital Chaplain   Accountants
  Engineers   Musicians
  Agriculturalists   Radio and Television
  Doctors   Specialists
  Nurses   Rescue Mission Director

Now go back and look at all the jobs you have listed. Pick
the five that seem most interesting to you.
  1.
  2.
  3.
  4.
  5.
On the following pages, complete the information requested
for each of the five jobs you listed.

Occupation _____

_____

Kind of Work—

Career Patterns—

Where People Are Employed—

Qualifications—

Employment Outlook—

Earnings and Working Conditions

Related Jobs—

Occupation _____

_____

Kind of Work—

Career Patterns—

Where People Are Employed—

Qualifications—

Employment Outlook—

Earnings and Working Conditions—

Related Jobs—

Occupation _____
_____

Kind of Work—

Career Patterns—

Where People Are Employed—

Qualifications—

Employment Outlook—

Earnings and Working Conditions—

Related Jobs—

Occupation _____

_____

Kind of Work—

Career Patterns—

Where People Are Employed—

Qualifications—

Employment Outlook—

Earnings and Working Conditions—

Related Jobs—

Occupation _____

_____

Kind of Work—

Career Patterns—

Where People Are Employed—

Qualifications—

Employment Outlook—

Earnings and Working Conditions—

Related Jobs—

Decision Making

Through this section, we are going to help you make some decisions about choosing a specific career. Up until now we have told you about many of the elements involved in career choice. We are now going to show you the entire process in a nutshell. Career choice involves three major processes: (1) Self-Exploration = Self-Knowledge; (2) Occupational Exploration = Occupational Knowledge; and (3) Matching Self-Knowledge with Specific Occupations. When choosing an occupation you must have knowledge about yourself, you must have knowledge of the available occupations, and you must be able to match this self-knowledge with specific occupations. Look at the following diagram depicting these three-stage processes in more detail.

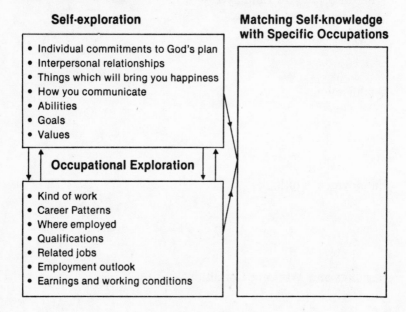

Self-exploration

- Individual commitments to God's plan
- Interpersonal relationships
- Things which will bring you happiness
- How you communicate
- Abilities
- Goals
- Values

Occupational Exploration

- Kind of work
- Career Patterns
- Where employed
- Qualifications
- Related jobs
- Employment outlook
- Earnings and working conditions

Matching Self-knowledge with Specific Occupations

Matching Process

We are going to show you how to match your self-knowledge and occupational knowledge with specific occupations. We are going to use a point accumulation procedure as given in the following paragraphs.

In chapter 2 you explored four kinds of interpersonal relationships. Each one of them is important to your mental well-being. They are listed below. We want you to rank them from one to four in order of importance. After doing this, we want you to assign a point value to each interpersonal relationship. The one that you rank number one should be given four points, number two should be given three points, number three should be given two points, and number four should be given one point.

Rank	Point Value	Interpersonal Relationship
_____	_____	People I can depend on in a pinch.
_____	_____	People who respect my competence.
_____	_____	People who share my concerns.
_____	_____	People who are close friends.

From chapter 1 you should list your four major commitments to God's plan. Rank them and assign a point value, number 1 receiving 4 points, number 2 receiving 3 points, number 3 receiving 2 points and number 4 receiving 1 point.

Rank	Point Value	Commitments
_____	_____	
_____	_____	
_____	_____	
_____	_____	
_____	_____	

Look at chapter two and find the five things which you believe will bring you the most happiness. We want you to list them in order of importance, the top one being listed first, and so forth.

Point Value		Things That Will Bring Me Happiness
5	1.	
4	2.	
3	3.	
2	4.	
1	5.	

You will notice that we placed a point value beside each one of the listings.

From chapter 2 list your top three abilities with the top ability being listed as number 1 the next ability number 2, and so on.

Point Value		Ability
3	1.	
2	2.	
1	3.	

From chapter 3 list your top five values in order of importance. The most important value should be listed as number 1.

Point Value		Value
5	1.	
4	2.	
3	3.	
2	4.	
1	5.	

From chapter 4 list your four goals in order of importance.

Point Value	Goals
4	1.
3	2.
2	3.
1	4.

Look at the scores in chapter 1 on communication styles. List the three communication styles below in order of importance.

Point Value	Communication Style
3	1.
2	2.
1	3.

As you can see, you have assigned point values to each of the areas that we have explored in chapters 1, 2, 3, and 4. This point of value will be applied to each of the five occupations that you have explored in depth. On each of the next five pages we want you to list the five occupations you have explored in depth and add up the point value for each occupation. Let us explain this in more detail. For example, let's say that one of the occupations you chose was accounting. You would list accounting at the top of the page beside the word "occupation." Next, add up the total point value for accounting. Here is how you do this:

Step 1: First decide which of the four interpersonal relationships will be best served by this occupation. Use your own best judgment. It may be a little vague and you will probably have to think this through carefully. Look back at the description of your chosen occupation. After you chose the *one* interpersonal relationship that will be best served, look at the point value beside the interpersonal relationship and place this point value below the occupation.

Step 2: Look at the list of things which will bring you most happiness and decide which one of the four things will be best achieved through this occupation. Again make your own best judgment. Your decision is based on your own evaluation. Look at the point value for this and place the point value below the occupation in the allotted space.

Step 3: For this occupation, decide which of your top three abilities will be most needed for this occupation. Look at the point value beside the ability and place it below the occupation in the allotted space.

Step 4: Look at your top five values. Decide *how many* of these values will be served by this occupation. All five may be served or only one may be served. Decide how many and look at the point value of each. Add these up and place the point value below the occupation in the allotted space.

Step 5: Look at your goals. Decide *how many* goals can be accomplished through this occupation. Again, all of them may be accomplished, or only one. Perhaps none of them will be accomplished. In any event, decide which of the goals will be accomplished (if any) and add up the point totals and place them in the allotted space.

Step 6: Look at your communication styles. Pick the communication style that you think is most important to this occupation. That is, which style do you think will be most used? Look at the point value and place it in the allotted space below the occupation.

Step 7: Add up all the point values and place them in the total points section. This is the total value for this occupation. *Do this for all five occupations.*

Occupational Assessment

Occupation _____

Points

Interpersonal Relationships _____

Things Which Bring Me the Most Happiness _____

Abilities _____

Values _____

Communication Style _____

Goals _____

Total Points _____

Occupational Assessment

Occupation _____

Points

Interpersonal Relationships   _____

Things Which Bring Me the Most Happiness   _____

Abilities   _____

Values   _____

Communication Style   _____

Goals   _____

                          Total Points   _____

Occupational Assessment

Occupation _____

Points

Interpersonal Relationships _____

Things Which Bring Me the Most Happiness _____

Abilities _____

Values _____

Communication Style _____

Goals _____

Total Points _____

Occupational Assessment

Occupation _____

Points

Interpersonal Relationships   _____

Things Which Bring Me the Most Happiness   _____

Abilities   _____

Values   _____

Communication Style   _____

Goals   _____

Total Points   _____

Occupational Assessment

Occupation _____

Points

Interpersonal Relationships _____

Things Which Bring Me the Most Happiness _____

Abilities _____

Values _____

Communication Style _____

Goals _____

Total Points _____

You have now completed point evaluations for five occupations. These occupations may or may not be the occupation for you, but if you have thoroughly examined the occupation in depth and have looked at yourself conscientiously, you should have a good idea of the direction you want to take. A word of caution here, *do not allow indecision to paralyze you.* Eventually you will have to choose an occupation. It will not be any easier to choose at a later date. *Career decision making is very hard work and if you are not willing to work at it you may never find a career which will help you achieve your full potential.*

We are going to ask you to list the five occupations below in order of their point value. If there is a tie, you should go back and reread the information about the two occupations and make a decision as to which one you think is most important. After listing each occupation, we are going to ask you to write one objective that will help you better understand this career and can be accomplished in the next six months. If you do not remember the purpose of an objective, look back and review chapter 4.

Occupation	Objective

1. _____   _____

                           _____

                           _____

_____

2. _____   _____

                           _____

                           _____

3. _____   _____

                            _____

                            _____

4. _____   _____

                            _____

                            _____

5._____   _____

                            _____

                            _____

6
Where Do I Go from Here?

Now you have come a long way, and if you have followed each of the exercises you have done a lot of work! But you have also selected five possible vocations. You have narrowed the field. And from examining your abilities, values, and goals as an individual, you have ranked each of the five occupations. If you have been honest in your self-assessment, then the top ranked occupation is probably the best for you. Now it is time to start working toward that occupation. We are suggesting that you adopt for yourself some short- and long-range goals that will help you start in that direction. We believe that development of career plans include three basic parts:

1. Deciding on an occupation.
2. Gaining the appropriate educational and work experience.
3. Developing a strategy for career search.

You have completed the first step by deciding on a career. Now it is important for you to start preparing yourself for that career.

You might remember one very special thing—be patient. Just because you have decided upon a career does not mean you can start tomorrow. There is first the basic training required for entering the career and then an appropriate internship in many occupations before you can be fully involved in your career. Now it is time to focus on the preparation involved.

Developing Career Plans

Once you have decided on the kind of occupation that you want to enter, you must then begin to develop the necessary skills for entry level employment. As defined earlier, *entry level* means the minimum amount of skills and experiences necessary before you can enter a job. In most cases people are required to only have the minimum entry level skills, but one has to be careful on focusing on only entry level skills. This could restrict your career. What you want to do is to expand your experiences and training as broadly as possible while attaining entry level skills so that you have additional skills in the long range development of your career. For instance, suppose you aspire to be a mechanical engineer initially but later on you want to become the manager of an engineering department in a large company. You find out the entry level of mechanical engineering is a college degree. You therefore attend college and earn a degree in mechanical engineering, the minimum education for entry level. However, while you were in college you took part in student government, took elective courses in management and leadership development, and worked part-time for an engineering firm. While the degree will assist you in getting the entry level position, the additional experiences and courses will help you progress to your ultimate goal at a faster pace.

In essence, developing career plans is the same as designing a marketing plan. Eventually you are going to have to sell yourself to an employer. You are going to have to convince someone to hire you and give you an opportunity to progress in an occupation. So, in developing your career plans you must keep awareness for opportunities to develop occupational skills.

Setting Goals

Now you are ready to start the process of preparing for your career. Assume your ultimate objective is to be a practicing physician with a specialty in pediatrics. It is important to keep that objective in mind but also to establish some intermediate goals that will need to be achieved to get there. Set those goals. For example, to get to that point you will need to gain the requirements for admission to medical school. That means a college degree, with very high grades. Second it will be necessary to complete medical school. Then will come an internship and finally a residency.

In the following space, take a moment to make a list of the things you will have to accomplish before you can enter the occupation you have chosen. Place beside that the amount of time it will take you to fulfill those requirements from today's date, and next to that a target date for completing that goal. We have provided a sample list of the person who wants to be a pediatrician, using the year 1979 as a beginning point.

GOAL	TIME REQUIRED	COMPLETION DATE
1. College education	4 years	Spring, 1983
2. Complete medical school	4 years	Spring, 1987
3. Complete internship	1 year	Spring, 1988
4. Complete residency	2 years	Spring, 1990

Using this as an example set your own goals in the space provided.

GOAL	TIME REQUIRED	COMPLETION DATE
1.		
2.		
3.		
4.		

At the same time you need to develop some immediate, short-term goals that will start you moving in the direction you want to go. A goal is made up of smaller parts that must be accomplished before the overall goal can be achieved. For example, in order to enter medical school you must have very high grades and certain courses that prepare you for medical school. A short-term goal can be taking a particular course you know is required or getting experience in part-time work that will be valuable to your learning process.

Take time now to make a list of immediate short-term goals that you can have accomplished in the next six months. In most cases these goals should help you achieve your first intermediate goal listed above.

Make a list of goals you hope to accomplish within the next six months.

1.

2.

3.

4.

5.

Now make a list of immediate short-term goals that you can accomplish in the next year.

1.

2.

3.

4.

5.

As you establish these immediate goals, you may want to talk to some resource people about those goals. For example, you can talk to a vocational counselor about what you need to be doing now. You may also want to consult a teacher in that field or someone you know that is in the field. You can gain valuable information from their experience that is not found in the textbooks. You may want to consult with your pastor at this point. He can help you set some realistic goals and he can help you understand how these goals can be a part of your overall Christian service.

Be careful how you view this preparation period. You will be tempted to view it as a necessary evil to be finished as quickly as possible. Remember career selection is a process. Take time to enjoy the preparation time. You can gain as much from it as from the career itself. Whatever field of work you choose, get involved now in the opportunities you have that will relate to your future career and in your personal Christian development. You do not have to wait to be involved in doing God's will.

Looking Ahead

You have selected a career. You have decided what you need to do to prepare yourself for that career. You have set some goals for yourself in order to start working in that direction. When you get close to the end of your preparation time, there will be some other matters to consider. Those considerations have to do with getting the right job, how to apply for that job, developing a resumé, and what to do in an interview. We are going to make some suggestions that will help you when you get to that point in your career development.

Developing Strategies for Career Search

Let's say you have decided on an occupation, developed the necessary educational training, involved yourself in other areas that expand your skills, and are not ready to pursue a job. You now have to know how to search for a job and get the one that you want. It has often been said that it is not necessarily the one who knows the most that gets the job, but the one who knows most *how* to get the job. A job search can be one of the most disheartening and traumatic experiences of your life. For employers to turn you down when you feel highly qualified is a blow to anyone's ego and can easily lead to settling for something less than your qualifications. Consequently, it is extremely important during a job search to remain optimistic. Don't let rejection shock you into changing your plans. Be tenacious. Don't give up. We will show you several ways to find a job and will help you develop the necessary marketing strategies. At the stage of job search you must be unrelenting in your pursuit.

Sources of Jobs

Once you know exactly what job you want to pursue, and this is extremely important to know, you are ready to identify the sources of jobs. You want to develop a list of specific job sources and those people who can help you in finding employment. When you develop this list of sources and begin to pursue employment, you should keep an optimistic attitude. You should not be afraid to ask. After all, if you believe you are basically a self-motivated and competent person, you should not be afraid to ask. If you don't believe you have something to offer a prospective employer, you need to reassess your job search.

We are going to suggest eight sources of jobs for you to consider in generating a list of sources.

1. *Friends and acquaintances.* Think of all the people you know who can help you find job leads. You will probably find that you have many people to talk with. Ask these people for help in pursuing a job. You don't have to ask them for a job and put them on the spot. You simply want to ask their advice and assistance. Often this approach can lead to many job interviews.

2. *Newspapers.* Newspapers have many job leads that you

may want to look into. If you have identified an area of the country in which you want to live, subscribing to a newspaper from that area can provide you with many possible job leads.

3. *Employment agencies.* For a fee, employment agencies will help you in securing employment. If you decide to go to an employment agency there are many things you must be aware of if you want to be successful. First, an employment agency makes its money by placing you in a job. Although the person at the agency may be called a counselor or some other name, you must remember that this person is essentially in sales. If you are not placed on a job the employment agency loses money. Therefore, when you walk through the door this salesperson is determined to place you in a job. If they do not currently have a job that you want, most agencies will try to sell you on some of the jobs they already have available. Do not become a victim by allowing the salesperson to sell you on a job that you do not want.

We recommend that you not use an employment agency until you have exhausted all the other alternatives we are suggesting. You stand to pay a high fee for finding a job, and unless you are adamant in what you want, you may inadvertently be talked into taking a job which you did not want.

4. *Management consulting firms.* These firms usually recruit for various companies and the company pays all fees for this. When you go to a management consulting firm, it is important to remember the firm is working for the company and not you. If you happen to fit the qualifications of a position they presently have open then you are in luck. If you don't, a management consulting firm is not going to give you much help. These firms are less likely to attempt to sell you on a job because they must find exactly what a company wants and send them that kind of person if they want repeat business.

5. *Professional and trade magazines.* Almost all professions or trades have a professional publication. Usually propsective employers advertise in these publications. They are excellent sources of jobs, depending upon your qualifications.

6. *Local companies.* Although you have probably been discouraged from randomly contacting companies, we believe this is perhaps the best source of information about jobs that you can find. If you know the geographical location of where you want to work, usually the local Chamber of Commerce can provide you with a list of companies. Assuming you know the kind of job you want, you can quickly narrow your list of companies.

7. *College placement centers.* Almost all colleges provide a placement service for its graduates. Even if you only attended for a short time and did not graduate, they will most often provide this service. Usually the service is either free or only a small fee is charged. This, we believe, is an excellent source of job leads if you have attended college.

8. *Professional and trade associations.* Almost all of these associations have an annual convention and during this time they usually provide a placement service for those attending. Since these people usually converge from all over the country, this is an excellent time to find employment.

Marketing Yourself to Prospective Employers

We have talked about the first step in seeking any kind of employment—locating the job. Once you've identified the sources, you must develop a marketing plan which will present you to prospective employers in the most positive light possible. Remember that when a prospective employer looks at your credentials, the first thing he will do is look for the aspects of your background that would eliminate you from the job. You do not want to build into your marketing plan anything that would be irrelevant or would eliminate you from an interview. On the other hand, *it is absolutely essential to be honest.* Do not distort the truth in any shape or form. Be straightforward at all times. If you are being considered for a responsible position, and you certainly want to be, any prospective employer will investigate thoroughly all the facts you have given him about yourself. If these facts are not substantiated, you have eliminated your chances of employment with this company, possibly for all time. Deception in a job search does not pay.

The objective of a job search after identifying sources of jobs is to get an interview. You want to talk directly with the employer so that you may tell him about your abilities. In some cases, you may be able to make a simple telephone call and get an appointment. For the more competitive jobs, usually jobs that require a higher level of experience and education, you may not be able to get an immediate appointment. This means you must present yourself on paper to a prospective employer who will then narrow his choice down to a few candidates for interviews. This means you will have to develop a summary of your education and experience in what is commonly called a *resumé*.

Briefly, the elements of marketing yourself to a prospective employer include: getting an interview through a telephone call or through a resumé, successfully interviewing, and following up. Let us go back over these marketing techniques and talk about them in more detail.

A *resumé* is simply a one- or two-page typewritten summary of your qualifications. This document is usually written for a specific kind of job and includes identifying data and information that may qualify you for a position.

In developing your resumé you should consider the following suggestions.

• Remember a resumé should be designed to get you an interview.

• A resumé should not exceed two pages, preferably it should be only one page.

• A resumé should include your name and address. It is illegal to ask a person their age, but you may want to put it on your resumé. There may be some biases toward age by employers. They may be looking for someone older or younger, and if you place your age on the resumé, you may be ruled out. Keep in mind, job performance is not always a function of age. You may be very competent to do a job at almost any age, and after the employer interviews, he may feel the same way. The main purpose of the resumé is to get an interview. Therefore, we do not recommend placing age on a resumé.

• We do not recommend that you place your current salary or how much money you want to make on your resumé. Save this for the interview or your cover letter. (We will talk about cover letters later.) Often salary is flexible for the employer. You want to make certain, however, that should you be employed, you will receive the highest possible salary for that position. If the employer thinks you will settle for less than the maximum, you may wind up on the short end. Salary should be the very last thing you talk about. You want to get the interview and the job first.

• Your education and experience should be on a resumé. If you are short on experience, you should write a brief description of what you did in your positions. If you want to emphasize your education it should be placed first on the resumé. If you want to emphasize experience it should be placed first.

• Never list references on your resumé.

• Any noteworthy accomplishments such as club memberships, offices held, grades, volunteer activities, and so forth, should be listed on your resumé.

Look at the sample resumé for an idea of what your resumé should look like.

Ralph Smith
333 Boardwalk
Dry Gulch, Texas 11111   Age (Optional)

(915) 367-7172   Marital Status (Optional)

Employment Objective: A position in sales

Education: BBA 1979 University of Texas
Major: Marketing

Experience

1977-1979   Sales Clerk   Smith Furniture Company

Assisted manager in developing and carrying out a sales campaign. Helped increase sales by 5 percent with this campaign.

Earned all college expenses through sales commissions. Received excellent evaluations from store manager.

1975-1977   Assistant Manager   Harold's Electronics
111 Dusty Lane
Dry Gulch, Texas

Assisted manager in ordering all products, in inventorying store, in keeping sales records, and in direct selling.

Educational
Achievements   Dean's Honor Roll   1977-1979
Resident of Student Marketing Association
Maintained 3.7 grade point average (4.0 scale)
Member of Student Government

Now we want you to develop your resumé using the suggestions and following the example given.

Resumé

Now we want you to develop another resumé the way you would want it to be if you were to achieve your job objective. Be realistic, do not develop it by an impossible standard. Remember to include the kind of education you think you should have, the kind of part-time or full-time work experiences, and the additional activities and accomplishments which you think would compliment your job objective.

Ideal Resumé

When your resumé is fully developed, you are then ready to make contact with an employer. You usually do this by a cover letter. As you send the resumé, you are to write a *creative* letter which adds to or complements your resumé. Make the cover letter as personal as possible. State your purpose in the very first sentence and then develop some of your ideas, and finally have a conclusion. Look at the following letter:

Mr. John Jones
ABC Corporation
Dry Gulch, Texas

Dear Mr. Jones:

I am applying for the sales position that you advertised. With four years experience and a degree in marketing, I believe I am well qualified to become a part of your sales team.

My past experiences and education have been very successful. All my work superiors will verify that I am resourceful, an excellent salesperson, extremely self-motivated, and able to work independently. I plan to make sales my career and have acquired the education and experience to do so.

I am looking forward to the opportunity of interviewing with you.

Sincerely,

Ralph Smith

As you can see this letter has an introduction, a paragraph expressing some of the positive aspects of the person, and a brief closing sentence requesting an interview.

If after a few days you have not received a reply, you may want to make a follow-up call to the prospective employer to make certain your resumé has arrived. We do not recommend a follow-up letter at this time.

Suppose you have developed your resumé, written a cover letter, and received an appointment for an interview. You have been successful in your search to this point and should be commended. It has taken skill and perseverance to do this. The big step is now coming—the interview. Before you arrive for the interview you should fully prepare yourself. You should know as much about the company as possible. You should know how you can contribute to this company. You should be well-versed on the particular position for which you are applying.

How you dress for an interview may have a great bearing on your getting the job. Remember the purpose of the interview is to get a job offer, not to prove your uniqueness or individuality through dress. We recommend that you dress conservatively because you do not know the personal biases of the prospective employer. Someone once said, "When going for an interview, look conservative and think maverick." Perhaps this should apply in any interview. Many highly-qualified people have been turned down for jobs because of their dress. Don't let this happen to you. Again, keep in mind your goal at this point is to get a job offer. If you are one of those who want to prove your individuality through dress and that is more important to you, go ahead and dress the way you feel most comfortable. You must be willing to accept the *consequences* should you not get the job.

Interviewing is perhaps the most difficult aspects of job search. All your hard work to get an interview comes down to your interaction for a brief time with a prospective employer. If you are able to sell him on hiring you, your career is on its way.

Yet, when you show up for an interview you are likely to be given an application to complete. Do not take this lightly. An application completed properly and in detail may give the prospective employer a clue to how well you pay attention to details. If you are sloppy in completing an application, the prospective employer may conclude that you will be sloppy in performing work for his company. If you have thoroughly prepared your resumé you should have most of the information you need to complete an application.

You've secured an interview, investigated the company thoroughly so you can have considerable information about it, completed an application, and you are now sitting in front of your prospective employer. How do you respond? What do you say? Look at the following tips.

• Always look the person in the eye. Don't look up, down, or away. Keep a strong eye contact. If you don't, you run the risk of missing something the interviewer is saying. You also may give the impression of not being interested.

• During the interview try not to act nervous. Act natural and be relaxed. An interviewer may rate you low if you act uptight under pressure. The company wants employees who can perform under pressure and if you can't do this in an interview you may not perform well for the company.

• Listen very attentively to the interviewer. Answer the questions directly. Be careful not to appear to skirt the question. Never try to second guess the interviewer or to bluff.

• Never talk about yourself for over a minute. Speak clearly and distinctly but appear spontaneous in your answers. Be as specific as possible.

• Don't argue with the interviewer or be overflattering. This will always work against you.

• Never volunteer negative information. For example, if an interviewer asks you for your biggest weakness, try to re-phrase it in a positive way. You may say something like, "If I had a weakness, it is trying to accomplish more that is expected in a shorter period of time." An answer like this tells the interviewer that you are a hard worker and structures your weakness into a positive trait. Again, never volunteer negative information about yourself.

• Give a complete answer to the interviewer's question.

Don't cause the interviewer to constantly ask the same question. Be as thorough as possible when you give an answer.

• Don't beg for a job. Present yourself as honestly and directly as possible, but don't beg for the job.

• Never criticize your former employer, teacher, or acquaintance. Even if the interviewer phrases questions to you that will make it easy to say something negative, you should never speak negatively of anyone in an interview. If you do, the interviewer may conclude that you would do the same thing to your new employer.

• If the interviewer invites questions, have several questions prepared in your mind. Don't pull out a notepad and read them. Ask questions about the nature of the job, what kind of person they are looking for to fill the position, what are the future plans of the company, and so on. You may even ask the interviewer what he likes about working for the company.

• Smile and be friendly. Don't be overly sullen or unhappy looking.

• Never, we repeat, *never* bring up salary until either the interviewer brings it up or you are given a job offer. Your main purpose at this time is to get a job offer, not to negotiate salary. If you seem overly concerned with salary before getting a job offer, the interviewer could conclude that this is your only interest. You first have to show the interviewer you are the person for the job.

• Try to understand the position of the interviewer. If you talk down to the interviewer this may rule you out. The interviewer must make an important decision that could cost the company if the decision is a bad one.

• If you have something you think may be a negative point, you should think of ways for rephrasing it into a positive point and then bring it up in the interview. If, for example, you are applying for a job just after graduation from college and are short on experience, this could go against you. Why not emphasize the fact that you have a good track record in education and are highly qualified by virtue of your educational background. What you may lack in experience, you make up in initiative and self-determination. Then emphasize how initiative and self-determination are perhaps the most important qualities necessary for high levels of achievement. Just because one has experience does not mean they have been highly achievement-oriented.

• Make sure at the end of the interview that you have communicated to the interviewer that you understand the company and would like to be a part of it.

Conclusion

As you have read through this book, you have seen some of the principles involved in choosing a career. Career choice is a lifelong pilgrimage that can be an exciting and rewarding adventure if you are able to understand and make use of all the complex elements involving career choice.

Career choice first involves understanding the commitments you have made to Christ. Knowing yourself is the second element that you must understand. This is the foundation you will build upon in your quest for full development of a clear focus in your values, a willingness to choose an occupation, and the courage to pursue your choice.

We hope you have worked through the exercises. If you have, you have already gained a great amount of insight. Now, it's time to act on the goals you have set.

Bibliography

Barnett, Henlee, *Christian Calling and Vocation,* Grand Rapids: Baker Book House, 1965.

Beardslee, W. A., *Human Achievement and Divine Vocation in the Message of Paul,* Naperville, Ill.: Allenson, 1961.

Bolles, Richard & Crystal, John, *Where Do I Go from Here With My Life,* New York: The Seabury Press, 1974.

Campbell, David, *If You Don't Know Where You're Going You'll Probably End Up Somewhere Else,* Niles, Illinois: Argus Communications, 1974.

Dauw, Dean, *Up Your Career,* Prospect Heights, Illinois: Waveland Press, Inc., 1977.

Dunphy, Philip, Austin, Sidney and McEneany, Thomas (Editors), *Career Development for the College Student,* Cranston, Rhode Island: The Carroll Press, 1973.

Elder, Carl, *Making Value Judgments: Decisions for Today,* Columbus, Ohio: Charles E. Merrill Publishing Co, 1972.

Ford, Murray J. S., *Church Vocations—A New Look,* Valley Forge: Judson Press, 1971.

Glasser, William, *Positive Addiction,* New York: Harper & Row, 1976.

Graves, Allen W., *Christ in My Career,* Nashville: Convention Press, 1958.

Hamacheck, Don E., *Encounters With the Self,* New York: Holt, Rinehart and Winston, 1978.

Hoppock, Robert, *Occupational Information,* New York: McGraw-Hill Book Company, 1967.

Hoyt, Kenneth, *Application of the Concept of Career Education to Higher Education:* An Idealistic Model, Washington, D. C.: U. S. Government Printing Office, 1976.

Kemp, Charles F., *The Pastor and Vocational Counseling,* St. Louis: Bethany Press, 1961.

Maslow, Abraham, *Motivation and Personality,* New York: Harper and Row, 1954.

Maston, T. B., *God's Will and Your Life,* Nashville: Broadman Press, 1964.

Million, Elmer G., *Your Faith and Your Life Work,* New York: Friendship Press, 1961.

Morley, Fenton, *The Call of God,* London: SOCK, 1959.

Pearce, J. Winston, *God Calls Me,* Nashville: Convention Press, 1958.

Rand, Willard J. Jr., *Call and Response,* Nashville: Abingdon Press, 1964.

Rogers, Carl, *On Becoming a Person,* Boston, Mass: Houghton-Mifflin, 1970.

Selye, Hans, *The Stress of Life,* New York: McGraw-Hill Book Company, 1956.

Sigsworth, John W., *Careers for Christian Youth,* Chicago: Moody Press, 1956.

Skinner, B. F., *Beyond Freedom and Dignity,* New York: Bantam Books, 1971.

Super, Donald, *Career Development: Self-Concept Theory,* New Jersey: College Entrance Examination Board, 1963.

Thompson, Melvin, *Why Should I Hire You,* Carlsbad, Calif.: Venture Press, 1975.

Toffler, Alvin, *Future Shock,* New York: Random, 1970.

Weatherhead, Leslie D., *The Will of God,* Nashville: Abingdon Press, 1944.

Weiss, Robert S., "The Fund of Socioability," *Transaction,* July/August, 1969.